Plant Powered Little People

A PRACTICAL GUIDE TO PLANT-BASED NUTRITION FOR UNDER-FIVES

Paula Hallam RD

Plant Powered Little People

©2023 Paula Hallam &
Meze Publishing Limited
First edition printed in 2023 in the UK
ISBN: 978-1-915538-22-2
Written by: Paula Hallam
Edited by: Katie Fisher
Photography by: Paul Gregory
Designed by: Paul Cocker & Phil Turner
PR: Emma Toogood & Lizzy Capps
Printed and bound in the UK by
Bell & Bain Ltd, Glasgow

Published by Meze Publishing Limited
Unit 1b, 2 Kelham Square
Kelham Riverside
Sheffield S3 8SD
Web: www.mezepublishing.co.uk
Telephone: 0114 275 7709
Email: info@mezepublishing.co.uk

Foreword

Twelve years ago, I changed my diet, moving to a natural, plant-based eating pattern in a bid to improve my health. It worked wonders for me. I fell in love with this approach to cooking and really enjoyed filling my plate with an array of colourful, flavourful ingredients.

Over time I became really confident in the kitchen and in my knowledge of how to look after my health, but as soon as I found out I was pregnant with my first daughter I knew there was a whole new world of information I needed to dive into. That's when I started following Paula, taking note of all the brilliant information she was sharing, equipping myself with everything I needed to create a nutritious diet for both my girls.

The girls are three and four now and we love cooking together. We've had fussier periods and easier periods when it comes to food; it's not a stress-free job feeding toddlers sometimes! I know I'm not alone in wondering exactly what I need to do to raise happy, healthy children though. So many families are thinking about eating more plants, moving to meat-free Mondays, a flexitarian approach or even a fully veggie or plant-based way of living. That's why this book is so brilliant.

Paula has created such an approachable, comprehensive guide for all parents, whatever your family's diet looks like. It's non-judgemental, easy to understand, and covers everything you'd ever need to know about your children's diets and nutrition. I wish I'd had that guidance earlier in my own parenting journey and I'm sure this book will be a huge help to so many people.

Ella Mills,
Founder of Deliciously Ella

Acknowledgements

I would like to say a sincere and heartfelt thank you to the Plant Based Kids community for all your support and encouragement – without you, I would not have considered creating this book for you.

To my husband Mark, for always supporting me and being my biggest cheerleader… you have always encouraged me to dream big and I am so grateful for your unwavering love and support.

To our girls, Lily and Maddie – thank you for being my inspiration and for your very honest feedback on my plant-based creations! Being your mum is the best gift in the world x

Thank you to my wonderful friends and colleagues, Ailsa and Lucy, who read the first draft of the book and provided helpful and constructive feedback. I am immensely grateful for your time, honesty and friendship.

To the team at Meze Publishing, for helping me turn my vision into a beautiful and informative book. Your expertise, patience and support has been incredible. Thank you so much; I am so grateful to all of you.

Paula Hallam x

About the Author

Paula Hallam is a registered children's dietitian, mum to two girls, and plant-based nutrition expert. Paula has been a dietitian for 24 years and has worked in the NHS for 18 years, including the world-famous Great Ormond Street Hospital for Children (twice!) as well as in the private sector, food allergy research, and providing nutrition consultancy to charities, food brands and childcare facilities.

Paula has worked as a nutrition consultant to many well-known brands including Deliciously Ella, Rhitrition, Babease, Wildly Tasty, Nature and Nurture, and Lune and Wild. Paula recently wrote a chapter on raising plant-based children in Deliciously Ella's latest bestselling cookbook, How To Go Plant-Based, which was published in August 2022.

Paula has an undergraduate degree in biochemistry and a postgraduate degree in Nutrition and Dietetics, as well as additional postgraduate training in paediatric nutrition and plant-based nutrition. In 2019, Paula completed a postgraduate certificate in Advanced Professional Practice in Paediatric Dietetics from the University of Plymouth and in 2021 completed the Plant Based Nutrition: A Sustainable Diet for Optimal Health course at the University of Winchester, accredited by the British Society of Lifestyle Medicine.

Paula is registered with the Health and Care Professions Council, a member of the British Dietetic Association (BDA) and Plant Based Health Professionals UK. She is a committee member of the Sustainable Diets Group of the BDA.

Paula has always had a love of cooking and delicious food. Growing up in Cape Town, she enjoyed spending time in the kitchen with her mum, learning favourite recipes and cooking skills from a young age. Nowadays, Paula enjoys cooking with her two teenage daughters and hopes to share her extensive knowledge of plant-based eating with a wider audience in Plant Powered Little People.

ABOUT THIS BOOK

Plant Powered Little People is designed to be a super-practical and easy-to-use guide to support your family's plant-based journey. The first half of the book gives you more information about the benefits of plant-based eating as well as detailed guidance on different nutrients: why they are important, what the best plant-based sources are, and how much your little one needs of each one. The last chapter of the book, before the recipes, is a practical guide to meal planning for your family, with special emphasis on under-fives, providing guidance on how and what foods to offer in order to provide all the nutrients discussed earlier in the book. Lastly, the super-easy recipes provide you with inspiration for delicious meals that the whole family can enjoy together, with plenty of adaptations for the littlest members of your family.

I am so excited for you to read this book… I have poured my heart into it using all my knowledge, passion and enthusiasm, and I hope that you will love it! – Paula

Contents

Breakfasts

Main Meals

Snacks

Dips

CHAPTER 1
Introduction

Chapter 1
Introduction

WHAT DOES 'PLANT-BASED' ACTUALLY MEAN?

Plant-based simply means diets or eating patterns that have "a greater emphasis on foods derived from plants" (1). By plants, I mean fruits, vegetables, wholegrains, nuts, seeds, pulses, and oils. Although many people may think that plant-based diets are the same as vegan or vegetarian diets, they are not. Plant-based diets don't have to be ONLY plants; they are eating patterns that consist of proportionately more foods from plant sources which can include vegan, vegetarian, pescatarian or flexitarian eating patterns. I have included a few definitions below to explain each of these.

VEGAN: excludes all animal products including meat, fish and seafood, poultry, eggs, dairy, and honey

LACTO-OVO VEGETARIAN: excludes meat, fish and seafood, and poultry but includes eggs and dairy products

OVO-VEGETARIAN: excludes meat, fish and seafood, poultry, and dairy products but includes eggs

LACTO-VEGETARIAN: excludes meat, fish and seafood, poultry, and eggs but includes dairy products

PESCATARIAN: excludes meat and poultry but includes fish and seafood, dairy products, and eggs

FLEXITARIAN: primarily vegetarian but may eat some meat, fish and seafood, poultry, dairy products, and eggs occasionally

Types of plant-based eating patterns

VEGAN · LACTO-OVO VEGETARIAN · OVO-VEGETARIAN · LACTO-VEGETARIAN · PESCATARIAN · FLEXITARIAN

WHY TALK ABOUT PLANT-BASED EATING FOR CHILDREN?

The most critical time for good nutrition is during the 1000-day period from conception until a child's second birthday (2), and the nutrition that babies and children receive in their early years has a profound effect on their later health (3). I think this time represents an ideal and unique opportunity to influence a child's health for the better, by offering a wide variety of plant-based foods right from the beginning of their eating journey, starting with their first bites of food when introducing solids from around six months of age. Research suggests that from the very earliest age, children's experiences with food influence their preferences as well as what they actually consume. What's more, the more varied a child's intake is, the healthier that child's diet is likely to be later in life (4).

Many studies have shown that preferences and eating habits form early during childhood and are likely to follow through until the beginning of adulthood (5).

In general, there has been a huge increase in the number of people turning towards plant-based diets as well as a heightened interest in how these eating patterns can not only improve our own health but also protect the health of our planet. According to The Vegan Society, the number of people following a vegan diet quadrupled from 2014 to 2019. In May 2021, they revealed that one in four British people had reduced the amount of animal products they were consuming since the start of the Covid-19 pandemic (6).

In its tenth year, Veganuary 2023 broke all previous records as over 700, 000 people worldwide signed up to participate in the month-long challenge of eating a vegan diet. It's clear that there are huge numbers of people who are keen to try out a vegan lifestyle, and many are sticking with it: according to the 2022 Veganuary statistics, 83% of participants who were not already vegan said they would be permanently changing their diet, either by becoming vegan or halving the amount of animal products they eat (7).

WHAT ARE THE BENEFITS OF PLANT–BASED EATING?

We know that plant-based diets offer many health benefits for adults as many studies have shown that plant-based diets can reduce the risk of developing many chronic diseases and increase the chance of living a longer and healthier life (8, 9). Healthy plant-based diets – based on whole foods and including wholegrains, fruits, vegetables, legumes, nuts and seeds – have been associated with a lower risk of chronic diseases such as heart disease, hypertension (high blood pressure), high blood lipids (such as LDL cholesterol – the 'bad' cholesterol) and type 2 diabetes (10).

There are also many health benefits of plant-rich diets for children, including the exposure to a wider variety of foods during childhood and adolescence, an association with children eating more fruits and vegetables, and a lower risk of obesity later in life (11). According to data from the National Child Measurement Programme in the UK, 10% of children aged four to five were obese in 2021/22 and a further 12% were overweight. In children aged ten to eleven, almost one in four (23.4%) were obese and a further 14.3% were overweight in 2021/22 (12). Studies have shown that vegetarian diets are associated with lower rates of obesity in adults and children. In addition, when compared to non-vegetarians, vegetarian children are leaner and the difference in BMI (body mass index) is more prominent in adolescents (13).

A study in 2021 looking at the growth, body composition, and cardiovascular and nutritional risk factors of omnivorous, vegetarian and vegan children between five and ten years of age (14) found that the vegan group of children had a lower risk of developing heart disease later in life than the other two diet groups. Similarly, in a VeChi study of six- to 18-year-olds (15), the vegan group of children had the lowest saturated fat intake and the highest intakes of polyunsaturated fats (PUFAs) which are associated with a lower risk of heart disease.

When we look at the information from these and other studies, eating patterns such as vegetarian and vegan diets certainly appear to be helpful in the long-term prevention of overweight and obesity. I think it's important to mention here that we don't yet have data from studies following children's health outcomes over many years; this is a gap that I think is likely to be filled with evidence and research in the years to come.

Fibre

There is strong evidence to suggest that diets high in fibre are associated with a lower risk of heart disease, strokes, type 2 diabetes, and bowel cancer. According to the 2015 report from the Scientific Advisory Committee on Nutrition, an adult should have 30g of fibre per day, with a proportionately lower recommendation for children from two years old (16). However, the latest National Diet and Nutrition Survey report showed that fibre intakes were below recommended values across all age groups (17). Adults between 19 and 64 years were eating just under 20g of fibre per day on average, while children were eating the following amounts on average: 10g per day between 18 months and three years old, 14g per day between four and ten years old, and 16g per day between 11 and 18.

The NHS recommends the following fibre intakes per day for children (18):

2-5 years: about 15g

5-11 years: about 20g

11-16 years: about 25g

Introducing more plant-based foods (fruits, vegetables, wholegrains, beans, lentils, nuts, and seeds) is a great way of increasing fibre intakes in children (and adults) which in turn can improve their long-term health. For babies and children between six months and two years of age, I recommend a gradual introduction of fibre. You can read more about this in Chapter 5 from page 99.

Fruit and Vegetables

It probably won't surprise you to hear that children in the UK are not eating nearly enough fruits and vegetables! Almost one third (29%) of children in the UK aged five to ten years eat less than one portion of vegetables per day, with those living in the poorest conditions eating the fewest vegetables (19). Less than one in five children (18%) between five and 15 years old eat five portions of fruit and vegetables per day in England, according to the Health Survey for England (20). Introducing fruits and vegetables (as well as legumes, nuts, seeds, and wholegrains) to children from an early age can help set up healthy eating habits for life, because familiarity helps young children to accept food more easily.

NOT ALL PLANT—BASED DIETS ARE CREATED EQUAL...

It's important to remember that eating a fully or mostly plant-based diet is no guarantee of good health, as the quality of the food itself still needs to be considered. For example, a plant-based diet consisting only of fried potato chips and highly processed meat alternatives may be classified as vegan, but certainly wouldn't be healthy! This was illustrated in a recent review which found that plant-based diets including higher amounts of refined grains and foods with added sugar had less favourable outcomes in terms of cardiovascular risk, whereas plant-based diets containing higher amounts of healthful plant-based foods such as wholegrains, fruits, vegetables, nuts, seeds, and legumes had more favourable cardiovascular risk profiles (21, 22).

There have been several other studies that support that same concept: an eating pattern that mostly consists of minimally processed whole foods – such as fruits, vegetables, wholegrains, legumes, nuts, and seeds – will result in more favourable health outcomes, such as maintaining a healthy weight over the long term, more favourable cardiovascular risk profiles, and a decreased risk of certain cancers, particularly bowel cancers (23, 24, 25, 26, 27, 28).

ARE PLANT—BASED DIETS SAFE FOR YOUNG CHILDREN?

The short answer is yes! But let me explain in a bit more detail…

Many professional organisations around the world agree that plant-based diets, including vegetarian and vegan diets, can be safe for children of all ages, as long as they are appropriately planned. Some of these organisations include the British Dietetic Association (BDA), The Academy of Nutrition and Dietetics, The American Academy of Paediatrics, The Canadian Paediatric Society, and Dietitians of Canada (29-33). The BDA says that a "balanced vegan diet can be enjoyed by children and adults, including during pregnancy and breastfeeding, if the nutritional intake is well-planned" while the Academy of Nutrition and Dietetics takes the following position: "appropriately planned vegetarian and vegan diets are healthful, nutritionally adequate, and may provide health benefits for the prevention and treatment of certain diseases. These diets are appropriate for all stages of the life cycle, including pregnancy, lactation, infancy, childhood, adolescence, [and] older adulthood" (30).

For the sake of balance and transparency, I think it's important to point out that there are some professional organisations around the world that don't recommend vegetarian and vegan diets for children, such as the German Nutrition Association, the German Society for Paediatric and Adolescent Medicine, the Spanish Paediatric Association, and the French-Speaking Paediatric Hepatology, Gastroenterology and Nutrition Group (34). In the European Society of Gastroenterology, Hepatology and Nutrition (ESPGHAN) Position Paper on Complementary Feeding, the group emphasises that vegan diets with appropriate supplements can support normal growth and development. ESPGHAN also recommends regular medical and dietetic supervision of children on vegan diets in order to avoid any possible negative outcomes (35). Although these organisations sound quite negative about plant-based diets for children, they all agree that "the successful provision of a nutritionally complete vegan diet for a child requires substantial commitment, expert guidance, planning, resources, supervision and supplementation" (35). So, I think we can all agree that careful planning is required but that's what this book is here to help you do!

When looking at research about plant-based diets, it is important to remember that children are not 'mini-adults' and the results from studies based on adults cannot automatically be applied to children. This is because children require more energy and nutrients per kilogram of body weight than adults, their nutritional requirements change throughout childhood, and they are also more vulnerable to nutritional deficiencies than adults (36, 37). When it comes to the safety of plant-based diets for children, it is important to consider not only their growth (see page 24) – which gives an indication of the overall adequacy of their energy/calorie and protein intake – but also their micronutrient (vitamins, minerals and trace elements) intake and how these nutrients are absorbed and used within the body.

Vitamins and Minerals

A study group called VeChi looked at the vitamin and mineral intakes of vegan, vegetarian and omnivorous children across two age groups in Germany; they found that vegan children had the highest intakes of many vitamins and minerals, such as the highest intake of vitamins E, K, B1, B6, folate and vitamin C as well as potassium, magnesium and iron (38). They also had the lowest intake of saturated fats and the highest intakes of polyunsaturated and monounsaturated fats (15, 39).

The studies also found that the vegan group of children had the lowest vitamin B12 intakes (without supplements). However, 97% of vegan children were taking vitamin B12 supplements and when these were taken into account, the vegan children had the highest vitamin B12 intakes. I recommend that all vegan children (and adults) are given a vitamin B12 supplement as plants are not a reliable source of vitamin B12. The VeChi study on the younger age group (38) found that the vegan children had the lowest calcium intakes, and that care should be taken to ensure young children have adequate calcium (and vitamin D) intakes to protect their bone health. An easy way to do this is to offer a calcium-fortified dairy alternative drink each day.

Iodine is another micronutrient that needs special consideration when planning a plant-based eating pattern. However, low iodine intakes are not only common in vegan diets, as illustrated in the VeChi studies, where iodine intakes were found to be low in all dietary groups (vegan, vegetarian and omnivorous), although they were lowest in the vegan and vegetarian groups (15, 38). The main sources of iodine in the UK diet are dairy products, eggs, white fish, and seafood. All vegan children should have a reliable source of iodine in their diet, whether from fortified foods (such as fortified dairy alternatives) or a supplement from one year of age.

Considering all these points, it is true there are certain vitamins and minerals that need special consideration when planning a fully plant-based diet for children. However, a nutritionally balanced diet is very achievable, as long as you are armed with accurate and practical information about children's nutritional requirements – which is what I'm here to help with! You can also check out Chapter 3 where I will cover lots of helpful information and practical examples of how to provide enough vitamin B12, calcium and iodine to children.

What about children's growth on vegan or vegetarian diets?

There is a lack of good quality studies and information about the association between vegetarian and vegan diets and children's health, including their growth. Many articles talking about children's growth on plant-based diets are based on old data from the 1980s, 1990s and early 2000s (37). Since then, many new plant-based food products have become available and our understanding of children's nutrition has grown enormously. However, there have been a few recent studies looking at children's growth on vegan diets. More recent studies about vegetarian and vegan children's growth include the 2019 VeChi study of one- to three-year-old German children (39), the 2021 Polish study of five- to ten-year-old children (14), and a Canadian study of six-month-olds to eight-year-olds (40).

In the VeChi study, they found that the vegetarian and vegan children grew equally as well as the omnivorous group of children, on average (39). However, it is important to mention that there were a small number of children in the vegetarian and vegan groups (2.4% and 3.6% respectively, versus 0% in the omnivorous group) who were significantly shorter, and 3.6% of the vegan group were considered underweight, compared to 0.6% of the omnivorous group and 0% of the vegetarian group. All the children who were considered short-for-age or underweight were either exclusively breastfed for extended periods of time without any solid foods being introduced or had insufficient total energy intakes. This highlights the importance of providing sufficient calories, fats and protein for all children to support their growth and development. Conversely, there was a higher percentage of children in the omnivorous diet group (23.2%) classified as overweight than in the vegetarian or vegan groups (18.1% and 18% respectively).

The Polish study found that vegetarian and vegan children were slightly shorter than omnivorous children, but also concluded that the height difference between vegetarian and omnivorous children was not statistically significant when other factors such as maternal and paternal height were taken into account, while vegan children remained slightly shorter than omnivorous children even when maternal and paternal height were taken into account (14). When looking at body composition data, vegetarian and vegan children tended to have lower body fat but similar levels of muscle (lean body mass) to omnivorous children. From this study, I would interpret this as the vegetarian and vegan children having an advantage in terms of body composition, as it is favourable to have more muscle (lean body) than fat mass in view of long-term health benefits.

In the Canadian study, they found no evidence of an association between vegetarian diets and growth as well as no difference in growth rates between children consuming vegetarian and non-vegetarian diets. The study did find that vegetarian children were slightly more likely to be underweight than non-vegetarian children and that children on a vegetarian diet were around 0.3cm shorter than the average three-year-old, which was not felt to be a meaningful height difference (40).

The results from all these studies illustrate that children following vegetarian diets can grow equally as well as children who include animal products in their diets if they are provided with enough calories to support their growth. As fat is the most energy dense of all macronutrients (which comprise fats, carbohydrates and protein), it is important to provide enough fats to young children to support their growth and development. I'll talk more about this in the next chapter as well giving you some practical examples of applying this knowledge to feeding young children.

Does my family need to be 100% plant-based to reap the health benefits?

The short answer is no! Studies have shown that shifting our eating pattern towards a more "plant-rich" diet can have a positive impact on our health, and it does not have to be an all-or-nothing approach. So, if your family would like a degree of flexibility in terms of including some animal foods, it is still possible to do this and reap the health benefits of a mostly plant-based approach.

Take the EAT-Lancet report. The EAT-Lancet commission involved 37 leading scientists from 16 countries around the world. These expert scientists were from many different disciplines – including human health, agriculture, political sciences and environmental sustainability – and their aim was to develop global scientific targets for healthy diets and sustainable food production. The EAT-Lancet report summarised the work of this group and stated that "a diet rich in plant-based foods and with fewer animal foods confers both improved health and environmental benefits". It also talked about the "planetary health plate" for adults, half of which is made up of fruits and vegetables with emphasis on wholegrains and sources of plant-based protein, and only 13% of the plate is made up of (optional) animal products such as meat, eggs, fish and dairy (41).

Another example is the eating patterns of the Blue Zones, five regions of the world with the greatest concentration of people who live to 100 years of age or beyond (centenarians). The eating patterns of these five regions (Okinawa in Japan, Ikaria in Greece, Loma Linda in California, USA, Sardinia in Italy, and Nicoya province in Costa Rica) are all very different but they have a few things in common; they are all around 85% plant-based with an emphasis on eating beans daily and only small amounts of meat (90-120g) four or five times per month (42).

At this point, I have a confession to make… my family and I are not 100% plant-based and I'm okay with that! My youngest daughter and I are vegetarian, while my older daughter and my husband are flexitarian (they usually eat meat once or twice a week). At home we all enjoy vegetarian foods together and when we are eating elsewhere, each person chooses what they would like to eat. This flexible approach works well for us, and I think it's important for each family to find an eating pattern that works for them. Some families may need or want a degree of flexibility, while others may find that a 100% plant-based eating pattern suits them; I'm here to support all families that would like to work towards a more "plant-rich" way of eating.

What's next?

In Chapters 2 and 3, we'll be taking a 'whistle stop tour' through children's nutrition, including key nutrients for children's growth and development and how to provide them from plant-based food sources.

CHAPTER 2
Macronutrients

Chapter 2
Macronutrients

Macronutrients are the nutrients that are required by our bodies in larger amounts (macro means big) and they provide children with the energy that they need to grow, thrive and support all bodily functions. The three macronutrients which provide energy are protein, carbohydrates and fat.

As they are growing and developing, children have unique nutritional requirements that change throughout childhood and adolescence. The first year of life represents a period of extremely rapid growth; on average babies triple their birth weight, grow 25cm in length and double their brain size, all within their first 12 months of life (1). Children also have higher energy requirements than adults relative to their body weight. For example, an average-size two-year-old needs around 1000 calories per day, which is 83kcal per kg, whereas adults need around 25-30kcal per kg on average (2).

PROTEIN

When it comes to protein and plant-based diets, the questions I'm asked usually focus on getting enough protein (quantity) and whether plant protein is as "good" as animal protein (quality). These are both key considerations which I'm going to discuss in detail here.

What is protein and why do children need it?

Protein is one of the macronutrients and is made up of amino acids, which are the building blocks of protein. When we eat foods containing protein, our bodies digest the protein and break it down into amino acids which are absorbed and used in the body to make different proteins such as hormones, enzymes, antibodies, and haemoglobin (3). There are thousands of different proteins with a multitude of different roles and functions in the body, involving many different organs such as the brain, immune system, gastrointestinal tract, and liver. Protein is also important for children's muscle, bone, skin, nail, and hair growth as well as the repair of muscles and tissues after injury and the tiny tears that occur during exercising, for example.

Protein is made up of amino acids that are the building blocks of protein; you can think of these as the bricks that make up the structure of a wall or building. There are 20 amino acids in total and all proteins are made up of different combinations of these. There are nine essential amino acids included in the total, known as such because the body cannot make them from other amino acids, meaning we need to obtain these from the foods we eat. The essential amino acids are isoleucine, leucine, valine, tryptophan, methionine, phenylalanine, histidine, threonine, and lysine (3).

How much protein do children need?

Age	RNI* (g/day)
0-6 months	12.5-12.7g
7-12 months	13.7-14.9g
1-3 years	14.5g
4-6 years	19.7g
7-10 years	28.3g
11-14 years	41.2g (females) 42.1g (males)
15-18 years	45.4g (females) 55.2g (males)
Breastfeeding / lactation (in addition to the adult female requirements of 0.75g protein per kg of bodyweight per day)	+ 11 (when baby is 0-6 months of age) + 8 (when baby is 6 months of age and over)

* RNI = reference nutrient intake

Is the quality of plant-protein as 'good' as animal protein?

It is a common misconception that plant foods are deficient in some of the amino acids, even though this has been proven false. All plant foods contain all 20 amino acids, including the essential nine, in varying amounts (5). This misconception likely stems from the fact that certain plant foods are lower in certain amino acids than the amounts required by the body. You often hear people say that plant foods are "missing" some of the essential amino acids, but it would be more accurate to say that the distribution of amino acids in some plant foods is not as optimal as it is in animal foods. For example, grains contain lysine and legumes contain methionine in lower amounts than the optimal amount for the human body, but this would only become an issue if you were eating a diet consisting of ONLY those foods, which is unlikely to be the case (6).

This may well be an issue in certain parts of the world where access to a variety of foods is a problem, but thankfully not in developed countries. As long as a reasonable variety of cereal foods, legumes (beans, lentils, soya foods), nuts, and seeds are eaten over a 24-hour period and sufficient calories are consumed, a child will be able to obtain all the amino acids they need for growth (6).

When you look at certain foods in isolation, animal foods do contain higher quantities of protein than plant foods by weight on average; see the table below. However, animal foods also come 'packaged' with more saturated fats than plant proteins and they contain no fibre.

NUTRIENT	IN 50G OF CHICKPEAS*	IN 50G OF BEEF*
Protein	3.5g	11g
Total fat	1.1g	6.8g
Saturated fat	0.1g	2.9g
Fibre	3g	0g

*Taken from an average of five brands

Animal Foods	Ingredient	Protein per 100g	Typical toddler portion	Protein per typical toddler portion
Meat	Beef mince, stewed	21.8g	40-50g	8.8-11g
	Chicken breast, casseroled	28.4g	40-50g	11.4-14.2g
	Pork chop, grilled	31.6g	40-50g	12.6-15.8g
Eggs	Chicken egg, boiled	12.5g	½-1 egg	3-6g
Fish	Salmon, grilled	24.2g	40-50g	9.7-12.1g
	Cod, baked	21.4g	40-50g	8.6-10.7g
Seafood	Prawns, boiled	22.6g	2-3 prawns	3.6-5.4g

Sources: 7, 8

Can children get enough protein on a plant-based eating pattern?

Yes, absolutely they can! In the VeChi study looking at 430 children aged one to three years of age, all diet groups (omnivorous, vegetarian and vegan) had protein intakes more than two times higher than the reference values (9). The omnivorous group had the highest protein intake of 2.7g per kg, the vegetarian group 2.3g per kg and the vegan group 2.4g per kg. This illustrates that vegan and vegetarian children can obtain more than enough protein from these eating patterns. On the other hand, it is important to point out that very high protein intakes in early childhood (10-15% of the total daily energy intake or more), particularly from animal-based protein, are not desirable, as this can lead to an increased risk of being overweight and obesity later in life (10).

In the latest UK National Diet and Nutrition Survey, reported daily protein intakes are much higher than the reference values detailed in the table on page 29 (11). For example, the average daily intake for children aged one and a half to three years was 42g, which is almost three times the recommended amount for this age group (4). So, children generally eat far more protein than they need. In most studies, the protein intakes of vegetarian and vegan children are compared to those of omnivorous children and found to be lower. However, when you look at that data against the background of children eating almost three times the recommended amount of protein, having a relatively lower intake can be seen as beneficial.

IN A NUTSHELL...

Recommended protein intakes are easy to achieve when following a plant-based eating pattern, as long as a reasonable variety of foods are eaten and sufficient calories are provided.

Plant Foods	Ingredient	Protein per 100g	Typical toddler portion	Protein per typical toddler portion
Pulses	Red lentils, boiled	7.5g	50-75g	3.8-5.7g
	Chickpeas, tinned	7.2g	50-75g	3.6-5.4g
	Peas, frozen and boiled	6g	25-50g (1-2 tbsp)	1.5-3g
	Peanut butter, smooth	22.6g	12g (thinly spread on 1 slice of toast)	2.7g
Beans	Red kidney beans, tinned	6.9g	50-75g	3.5-5.2g
	Black-eyed beans, boiled	8.8g	50-75g	4.4-6.6g
	Baked beans	5.2g	50-75g	2.6-4g
Tofu	Tofu, steamed	9g	40-50g	3.6-4.5g
Quorn®	Quorn® mince	13g	40-50g	5.2-6.5g
Soya (Texturised Vegetable Protein)	Soya mince	17g	40-50g	6.8-8.5g
Nuts (ground)	Almonds	21.1g	1-2 tbsp	1.3-2.6g
	Cashews	20.5g	1-2 tbsp	1.2-2.5g
	Walnuts	14.7g	1-2 tbsp	0.9-1.8g
	Hazelnuts	14.1g	1-2 tbsp	0.9-1.8g
	Brazil nuts	14.1g	1-2 tbsp	0.9-1.8g
	Pistachios	17.9g	1-2 tbsp	1.1-2.2g
	Pecans	9.2g	1-2 tbsp	0.6-1.1g
	Macadamias	7.9g	1-2 tbsp	0.5-1g
Seeds	Chia seeds	18g	1 tsp	0.6g
	Hemp seeds	35g	1 tsp	1.1g
	Sesame seeds	18.2g	1 tsp	0.7g
	Sunflower seeds	19.8g	1 tsp	0.6g
	Pumpkin seeds	24.4g	1 tsp	1g
Grains and starchy foods	Basmati rice, boiled	2.6g	Around 80g	2.1g
	Pasta, boiled	3.3g	Around 80g	2.6g
	Quinoa	4.7g	Around 80g	3.8g
	Oats, cooked in water	1.4g	Around 100g	1.4g
	Wholemeal bread	9.4g	½-1 slice	2-4g
	Potato, boiled	1.8g	¼-½ a medium potato	0.6-1.2g
	Pearl barley, boiled	2.7g	Around 80g	2.2g

Sources: 7, 8

CARBOHYDRATES

WHAT ARE CARBOHYDRATES?

Foods that are high in carbohydrates are often vilified and labelled as being bad, but these foods are a vital part of children's diets and provide many important nutrients for children such as energy, fibre, vitamins (particularly B vitamins), and minerals (particularly iron, zinc and calcium).

The word 'carbohydrates' encompasses both sugars and starches, so foods including table sugar, honey, fruit, rice, bread, pasta, potatoes, and porridge oats all contain significant amounts of carbohydrates. Most of these foods are a combination of carbohydrates, fats and proteins (except table sugar), as individual foods rarely contain only one nutrient. For example, potatoes are a good source of carbohydrates and are often thought of as a 'carb'. However, as well as being a good source of carbohydrates, potatoes also contain significant amounts of protein (3-4g of protein per 100g), a small amount of fat, and B vitamins. Similarly, pasta is a good source of carbohydrates and contains significant amounts of protein (almost 6g protein per 100g of cooked pasta) plus a small amount of fat and B vitamins. Remember, we eat foods not individual nutrients!

Why do children need carbohydrates?

Carbohydrates are the body's preferred fuel source; in other words, they provide energy to the body. In fact, virtually every cell in our body uses glucose from carbohydrates as their primary fuel. Carbohydrates are also a source of fibre – from wholegrains, which also provide a significant source of protein (12) – as well as B vitamins and minerals such as calcium, iron and zinc. Biochemically, carbohydrates can be described as molecules containing carbon, hydrogen and oxygen atoms in a ratio of 1:2:1 and of varying chain lengths. But I don't want to give you a biochemistry lesson! I think it is helpful to think of carbohydrates as an energy-giving nutrient. The carbohydrate chains are broken down into glucose in the body, which is the main fuel for every cell in the body.

Different types of carbohydrates

Carbohydrates can be broadly divided into two groups: sugars and starches. Sugars can be further divided into 'simple' sugars (the scientific term is monosaccharides) and more complex sugars, which we'll go into below.

MONOSACCHARIDES: Saccharide means sugar in Greek and 'mono' means one, as they consist of one molecule. Examples include glucose, galactose and fructose.

DISACCHARIDES: 'Di' means two, as these are made up of two monosaccharides. Examples include maltose (two glucose molecules) which is found in foods like wheat, barley and sweet potatoes; lactose, (glucose + galactose) which is the sugar in cow's milk; and sucrose (glucose + fructose) which is more commonly known as table sugar.

OLIGOSACCHARIDES: 'Oligo' means a few and oligosaccharides are found in many fruits, vegetables, grains like wheat and rye, and beans.

POLYSACCHARIDES: 'Poly' means many, as these contain thousands of glucose molecules linked together in chains. Examples of polysaccharides include starch, found in cereal grains and starchy vegetables; glycogen, the human body's storage form of glucose found in our muscles and liver; and cellulose, found in root and leafy vegetables, legumes, and some fruits such as apples and pears.

What are free sugars?

Public Health England defines the term free sugars as "any sugar that has been added to a food or drink by the manufacturer plus sugars naturally present in honey, syrups and unsweetened fruit juices" (13). Sugars naturally present in milk and milk products (lactose) as well as sugars naturally present in the cellular structure of foods are excluded and not considered free sugars.

In the Scientific Advisory Committee on Nutrition (SACN) report on carbohydrates from 2015, it was recommended that the maximum amount of free sugars should be no more than 5% of the energy intake for all adults and children over the age of two years (12). So, for a three-year-old, the average daily energy intake is 1300 calories, 5% of which is 65 calories, which equates to 16g of free sugars per day.

What is fibre?

Fibre is a type of carbohydrate that is not digested in the stomach or small intestine and therefore reaches the large bowel (colon) where it is fermented by bacteria to produce helpful chemicals for the body. Fibre has many benefits for the human body including preventing constipation, keeping you feeling full for longer, and feeding beneficial gut bacteria.

What about fibre for children?

There are no recommendations for fibre for children and babies under the age of two years. We know that fibre is important for gut health, but I recommend a gradual introduction from starting with solids up to two years of age. This is because babies and young children need nutrient- and energy-dense foods and fibre can fill up their tummies very quickly. In practice, I recommend that parents offer a combination of refined or 'white' carbohydrates and complex carbohydrates to their babies. For example, you can offer white pasta on some days and wholewheat pasta on other days. Remember that fruits, vegetables, beans, and lentils all contain fibre too (as well as cereals such as oats and wheat) so offering your baby a range of these foods is ideal.

Once they are over two years old, the NHS recommends the following amounts of fibre for children:

2-5 years = 15g per day

6-10 years = 20g per day

11-18 years = 25g per day

The recommended fibre intake for adults is 30g per day but on average, adults in the UK consume about 18g of fibre per day. Similarly, according to the latest National Diet and Nutrition Survey (NDNS), children in all age groups were not eating enough fibre. Their average fibre intakes were 10.4g, 14.3g, and 16g per day for ages 18 months to three years, four to ten years and 11 to 18 years respectively (11). As you can see from this information, we could all benefit from eating more fibre.

How much fibre is in different foods?

Food	Portion	Fibre Per Portion
Jacket potato (with skin)	1 small potato	2g
Wholemeal bread	1 slice	2.5-3.5g
Red lentils, cooked	3 tbsp	2g
Red kidney beans, tinned	3 tbsp	4g
Chickpeas, tinned	3 tbsp	2g
Weetabix-type cereal	20g (1 'biscuit')	2g
Porridge oats (dry)	25g	2g
Apple	½ an apple	1g
Raspberries	10 raspberries	2.7g
Carrot	½ a carrot	2g
Chia seeds	1 tsp	1.2g
Avocado	¼ of an avocado	2g
Peanut butter	1 tbsp (on 1 slice of toast)	1.2g
Hummus	2 tbsp	2.5g

Source: 7

So, can children have too much fibre? Yes, they can. Babies and young children have small tummies and if they have too much fibre, they can become full too quickly without receiving all the nutrients and energy that they need to grow and develop. Aim to offer a variety of refined or 'white' carbohydrates and wholegrains, introducing wholegrains gradually.

HOW CARBOHYDRATES AND FIBRE RELATE TO PLANT-BASED EATING

Plants are the only source of fibre in our diet, as animal foods do not contain fibre. Examples include fruits, vegetables, wholegrains (such as oats, wholewheat bread, brown rice, quinoa, and bulgur wheat), beans, lentils, nuts, and seeds.

In a VeChi study, the vegan group had the highest carbohydrate intake (56.2% of their total energy intake) while vegetarian children had the next highest intake at 54.1% of their total energy and the omnivorous children had the lowest carbohydrate intake (50.1% of their total energy intake). Fibre intakes followed a similar pattern, with vegan children consuming the highest amounts at 21.8g, vegetarian children 16.5g and omnivorous children 12.2g fibre per 1000 calories (14). This data illustrates that intakes of carbohydrates and fibre are not a problem in children with plant-based or mostly plant-based eating patterns. In fact, as outlined above, vegan and vegetarian children tend to eat more carbohydrates and fibre than omnivorous children.

IN A NUTSHELL...

Young children need nutrient- and energy-dense foods.

Carbohydrates are an important source of energy for young children.

Carbohydrate-rich foods also provide protein, B vitamins and minerals.

Fibre is important for children's long-term health but be careful not to overdo it for young children, as fibre can fill up little tummies before they have had enough calories to support their growth.

FATS

WHAT ARE FATS?

Fats are one of the macronutrients that provide the body with energy. Fats are the most energy-dense nutrient, providing nine calories per gram, compared to protein and carbohydrate which provide around four calories per gram. Fats are important for children as they provide energy needed for growth and development as well as helping with the absorption of fat-soluble vitamins. Fats have different health effects on the body, depending on the type of fat that is eaten.

WHAT ARE THE DIFFERENT TYPES OF FATS?

There are two main types of fats: saturated and unsaturated. Unsaturated fats can be further divided into polyunsaturated and monounsaturated fats. Biochemically, the difference between saturated and unsaturated fats is in the number of double bonds between the carbon atoms. Saturated fats have no double bonds whereas unsaturated fats have at least one (mono) or many (poly) double bonds between the carbon atoms. What this means practically is that saturated fats are solid at room temperature (think butter, lard, suet, and coconut oil) and unsaturated fats are liquid at room temperature, like most oils. High amounts of saturated fats are also found in foods such as chocolate, biscuits, cakes, pastries, cheese, cream, fatty or processed meats, ice cream, coconut milk and cream, coconut oil, palm oil, butter, ghee, suet, and lard.

Foods usually contain a mixture of saturated and unsaturated fats and in general plant foods contain a higher amount of unsaturated fats (coconut oil and palm oil being the exceptions) than animal foods. For example, nuts, seeds and avocados contain mostly unsaturated fats with small amounts of saturated fats, as illustrated by the table overleaf.

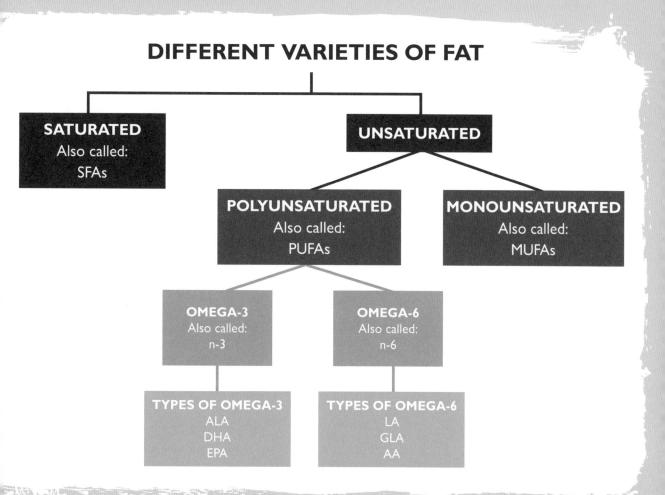

DIFFERENT VARIETIES OF FAT

- **SATURATED**
  Also called:
  SFAs

- **UNSATURATED**
  - **POLYUNSATURATED**
    Also called:
    PUFAs
    - **OMEGA-3**
      Also called:
      n-3
      - **TYPES OF OMEGA-3**
        ALA
        DHA
        EPA
    - **OMEGA-6**
      Also called:
      n-6
      - **TYPES OF OMEGA-6**
        LA
        GLA
        AA
  - **MONOUNSATURATED**
    Also called:
    MUFAs

DIFFERENT TYPES OF FATS IN PLANT FOODS (PER 100G)

Food	SFA (G)	MUFA (G)	PUFA (G)
NUTS			
Almonds	3.8	31.6	12.3
Brazil nuts	17.4	22.4	25.4
Cashews	9.5	27.8	8.8
Hazelnuts	4.6	49.2	6.6
Macadamias	11.2	60.8	1.6
Peanuts (actually legumes)	8.7	22.0	13.1
Pecans	5.7	42.5	18.7
Pistachios	7.4	27.6	17.9
Walnuts	7.5	10.7	46.8
SEEDS			
Chia	3.2	2.2	27.4
Hemp	4.7	5.6	36.8
Flaxseed (linseeds)	4.1	7.7	12.1
Pumpkin	7	11.2	18.3
Sunflower	4.5	9.8	31.0
Sesame	8.3	21.7	25.5
FRUITS			
Avocado	4.1	12.1	2.2
Coconut milk (tinned)	16.6	1.2	0.3

Sources: 7, 8

SFA = saturated fats

MUFA = monounsaturated fats

PUFA = polyunsaturated fats

Eating high amounts of saturated fats is associated with adverse health outcomes in adults, such as an increased risk of cardiovascular diseases. Although cardiovascular diseases generally present later in life, there is evidence that fatty deposits in arteries can start much earlier in childhood (15).

Studies have shown that replacing saturated fats with MUFAs and PUFAs wherever possible is helpful in reducing total and LDL cholesterol levels, both of which have been linked to increased risk of heart disease (15). What this means practically is regularly including foods such as nuts, seeds, avocado, olive oil, and rapeseed oil in your diet while trying to minimise ultra-processed foods such as biscuits, cakes and pastries. It also means reducing animal-based foods, though each family will have their own priorities and personal feelings about what animal products, if any, to include in their family's eating pattern. I think what is most important is trying to include more plants, which may mean eating 100% plant-based for some and a more flexible approach for others.

HOW MUCH FAT DO CHILDREN NEED?

Fats tend to get a lot of bad press generally, but they are actually a very important source of energy, especially for babies and young children under the age of five. Foods containing fats are also an important source of fat-soluble vitamins for children. The amount of total fat recommended in the diet is less than 35% of the total energy intake for children over the age of five and adults, with less than 11% of the total energy coming from saturated fats (14).

For children four years of age and younger, there are no specific recommendations to limit fat intakes. Breast milk contains approximately 4g of fat in total per 100ml, which means that around 50% of the calories in breast milk are derived from fats. From introducing solids at around six months until the age of four, children's fat intakes should be gradually decreased so that by four to five years of age, only about 30-35% of their total energy intake is coming from fats. Practically, this means that babies and young children under four years of age should be offered a source of fats with most or all of their meals. Plant-based eating patterns (especially vegan diets) can be lower in fats than diets including meat and other animal products, because foods such as legumes, fruits and vegetables are mostly low in fats.

For plant-based children, sources of good fats such as avocado, ground nuts or nut butters, seeds or seed butters, and plant oils such as olive or rapeseed should be proactively included in their meals to ensure they have enough fats in their diets. Fats have many important functions in the body, including fat-soluble vitamin absorption (vitamins A, D, E and K), hormone production, the provision of essential fats, and as an important energy source.

What does the research say about fat intakes in plant–based children?

In the VeChi study of one- to three-year-olds, all three groups of children (omnivorous, vegetarian and vegan) had similar total fat intakes as a percentage of total energy, between 32.6 and 33.7% (16). However, when looking at the different types of fats or the fat quality of the diet, the vegan children had the most favourable profile, followed by the vegetarian children. The vegan children had the lowest intakes of saturated fats and the highest intakes of PUFAs and MUFAs. There was a similar finding in the VeChi study of six- to 18-year-olds, with the vegan children showing the lowest saturated fat intakes and the highest intakes of PUFAs and MUFAs. This was further demonstrated biochemically, with blood results showing that the vegan group of children had the lowest serum total cholesterol and LDL cholesterol concentrations (14). Another study published in 2021 also found that vegan children had more favourable levels of blood fats (lower total and LDL cholesterol concentrations) than omnivorous children (17).

High levels of total and LDL cholesterol have been linked to an increased risk of heart disease and strokes. The formation of plaques (hard, waxy substances) in arteries and the subsequent narrowing of arteries (known as atherosclerosis) increase the risk of heart attacks and strokes (18). There is evidence that atherosclerosis starts in childhood (15) and therefore it is important to start minimising the risks of cardiovascular disease early on in life. We can do this by reducing foods that are high in saturated fats and focusing on foods high in polyunsaturated and monounsaturated fats.

In a nutshell...

Fats are an important source of energy for babies and young children.

Babies and young children need more fat than adults (as a percentage of their calories).

Aim to offer a source of fats at all or most of your child's meals and snacks.

Offer as much variety as you can, including nuts, seeds, avocado, olive oil, rapeseed oil, and (less frequently) coconut oil, cream or milk.

Avoid low-fat products for young children.

What are essential fats?

Essential fatty acids are fats that our bodies cannot make from other fats and therefore we need to obtain a source of these fats from the foods that we eat (19). There are two essential fatty acids: linoleic acid (LA) and alpha-linolenic acid (ALA). LA is also called an omega-6 type of fat, due to the position of the last double bond being six carbons from the omega end of the fatty acid molecule. Similarly, ALA is also called an omega-3 type of fat due to the position of the double bond being three carbons from the omega end of the fatty acid molecule (20).

Omega-3 fats are part of a group of fats called long chain polyunsaturated fats (LCPUFAs). There are three main types of omega-3 fats, known as alpha-linoleic acid (ALA), eicosapentaenoic acid (EPA), and docosahexaenoic acid (DHA). The human body can convert ALA to EPA and DHA through a series of steps. However, this process is not very efficient in humans. Studies have shown that only 5-16% of ALA is converted to EPA and <0.5-1% of ALA is converted to DHA (21, 22). In addition, if we include lots of omega-6 fats in our eating pattern, this can decrease the conversion of ALA to EPA and DHA as the processes compete for the same enzymes. There are also certain vitamins and minerals that are needed as 'helpers' (co-factors) for the enzymes, so including foods that are rich in vitamins and minerals is beneficial.

LA is widely distributed in many types of foods such as sunflower, safflower, soybean, peanut, and corn oils as well as certain nuts and seeds, particularly peanuts, sunflower seeds and sesame seeds. So, it is very easy to obtain enough LA from our diets and in fact, research shows that many people are eating too much of it, as the oils high in LA tend to be found in ultra-processed foods such as cakes and biscuits (20).

ALA is not as widely distributed within foods as LA. Plant-based sources of ALA include chia, hemp and flax seeds (and their oils) as well as walnuts and tofu. DHA and EPA are found mainly in oily fish and seafood as well as micro algae; oily fish have high levels of DHA and EPA because they eat micro algae! If your family includes eggs in their eating pattern, they are another possible source of omega-3 fats (particularly DHA) if the hens have been fed an omega-3 rich diet. Please note that not all eggs are a good source of DHA as it depends on what type of feed the hens have been given (23).

If your family includes some animal products, oily fish are an excellent source of essential fats DHA and EPA. Aim to include one portion of oily fish per week, if this is part of your family's eating pattern. Examples of oily fish include salmon, mackerel, sardines, anchovies, and herring (24).

Why are DHA and EPA so important?

Studies have shown that EPA and DHA have specific health benefits for the prevention of heart disease and a decreased risk of cognitive decline (loss of brain function) in later life (26). DHA is also considered a critical nutrient for babies and young children as it plays a crucial role in brain and eye development. In fact, 40% of the fats in a baby's brain are made up of DHA! Studies have shown that DHA is important for a baby's ability to learn, their memory and for supporting normal IQ (21). Babies receive DHA and EPA from their mother before birth (via the placenta) and from breast milk after birth, if the mother's diet contains adequate sources of DHA and EPA, or from formula milk supplemented with DHA and EPA.

Can children get enough essential fats from a plant-based eating pattern?

As mentioned above, there are several plant-based sources of ALA (chia, flax and hemp seeds, walnuts, and tofu). However, the conversion of ALA to DHA and EPA is not very efficient, especially if the intake of omega-6 fats is very high since the two fats compete for the same enzymes (24). Although the research about supplementing vegan and vegetarian adults with DHA and EPA is inconsistent, it suggests that there are certain vulnerable periods in life when supplementing with DHA and EPA would be beneficial. These periods are during pregnancy and breastfeeding, from birth to the age of two, and in elderly life. I recommend an algal oil supplement for these groups.

How much DHA and EPA to give: (25, 26)

Under 2 = 10-12mg per kg per day DHA

2-4 years = 100-150mg DHA + EPA per day

4-6 years = 150-200mg DHA + EPA per day

6-10 years = 200-250mg DHA + EPA per day

Breastfeeding: 400-500mg DHA + EPA per day (with at least 250mg being DHA)

In a nutshell...

If your family does not include oily fish or omega-3 enriched eggs in your weekly meal plan, consider an algal oil supplement to provide DHA and EPA.

The above is especially important for babies and children under the age of two, as well as during pregnancy and breastfeeding.

Include daily sources of ALA in your eating pattern, such as chia, flax or hemp seeds, walnuts and rapeseed oil.

CHAPTER 3
Micronutrients

Chapter 3
Micronutrients

Micronutrients are just as important as macronutrients, but they are needed in smaller quantities (micro means small). The World Health Organisation (WHO) defines micronutrients as "vitamins and minerals needed by the body in very small amounts. However, their impact on a body's health is critical, and deficiency in any of them can cause severe and even life-threatening conditions" (1). I know this definition sounds a bit scary, but the point is that although these nutrients are only required in tiny amounts (sometimes only microgram quantities) they are still vitally important to our health and wellbeing. You could say they are small but mighty!

VITAMIN AND MINERAL INTAKES IN PLANT-BASED CHILDREN

Plant-based diets are often demonised in the press as being deficient in various vitamins and minerals but in truth, plant-rich diets are abundant in so many nutrients, including micronutrients!

A VeChi study of one- to three-year-olds found that the vegan group of children had a more favourable overall vitamin and mineral intake, followed by the vegetarian group (2). The vegan children (without supplements) had the highest intakes of vitamins E, K, B1, B6, C, and folate, whereas the omnivorous children had the highest intakes of vitamins B2 and B12. In terms of minerals, the vegan children had the highest intakes of potassium, magnesium and iron, whereas the omnivorous children had the highest intakes of calcium and iodine. It is important to note that although omnivorous children had the highest intakes of iodine, all three groups had inadequate iodine intakes that were below the recommended value for iodine. When supplements were taken into account, the vegan group had the highest intakes of vitamins B12 and D.

VITAMINS

There are 13 essential vitamins that we need to stay healthy, with many different and diverse functions in the body. Our bodies cannot make most vitamins (or cannot make enough) and so we need to obtain them from the foods we eat.

Our bodies are able to produce certain vitamins themselves; vitamin D can be synthesised in the skin with the help of sunlight, niacin (one of the B vitamins) can be synthesised from an amino acid called tryptophan, and vitamin K and biotin (another of the B vitamins) are produced by bacteria in the gut. However, it is thought that we still need a supply of these vitamins from food as our bodies don't necessarily produce enough to keep us healthy (3).

There are two different types of vitamins: fat-soluble vitamins and water-soluble vitamins. Fat-soluble vitamins are vitamins A, D, E and K. Their absorption is improved if they are eaten with foods that contain fat. As fat-soluble vitamins can be stored in the liver, there is the potential for toxicity if too much of any of these vitamins is taken up by the body. Therefore, upper limits have been set for these vitamins to ensure a safe intake that is not excessive.

Although all vitamins are important for babies and young children, some are of particular importance during this period of growth and development, as well as certain vitamins that are not as abundant in plant-based eating patterns, so I will be looking at vitamins D, A, B12 and B2 in this chapter.

VITAMIN D

WHAT IS VITAMIN D AND WHY IS IT IMPORTANT?

Vitamin D is a fat-soluble vitamin that we can get from a few foods and is also produced by the action of sunlight on our skin; around 80% of our vitamin D comes from the latter with the other 20% being obtained through food (3).

Vitamin D is involved in maintaining bone health as it promotes the absorption of calcium from the gut. It also has many other roles, as the vitamin D receptor has been found in almost every tissue in the human body (4). For example, vitamin D decreases inflammation in the body and is involved in the healthy functioning of the immune system, cell growth and neuromuscular function (5).

The way that our body produces vitamin D is through the action of the sun's UVB rays on our skin, which converts 7-dehydrocholesterol to vitamin D in two steps. The vitamin D travels to the liver and then the kidney where it is converted into the active form of vitamin D, called 1,25-dihydroxyvitamin D or cholecalciferol. The sunlight has to be a specific wavelength to be effective at penetrating the skin and converting 7-dehydrocholesterol to vitamin D (5, 6).

Factors such as the amount of melanin (pigment) in our skin, our clothing, the season, latitude, time of day, cloud cover, air pollution, and sunscreen all affect the amount of UVB radiation that can reach the skin (6). What this means practically is that in the UK, we cannot produce enough vitamin D from October to the beginning of April, so a vitamin D supplement is recommended during this period for all adults and children over the age of five (see recommendations for under-fives below) because it is very difficult to obtain enough vitamin D from the foods we eat (even if your diet includes oily fish) and sun exposure at the correct wavelength is minimal during the winter months in the UK (6).

IS IT 'BETTER' TO TAKE VITAMIN D3 OR VITAMIN D2?

There are two different types of vitamin D: D2 and D3. Vitamin D3, also known as cholecalciferol, is the type of vitamin D that is formed when our skin is exposed to sunlight UVB rays. Vitamin D2, also known as ergocalciferol, is synthesised when plants and fungi are exposed to UVB rays (7).

There is some controversy about the absorption of vitamin D2 and D3 in terms of which one is more effective at raising vitamin D levels in the blood (called 25-hydroxy-vitamin D), partly because results from studies looking at this have been inconsistent (6). Some studies have shown that vitamin D3 seems to be more effective at raising 25(OH) vitamin D levels in the blood than vitamin D2, while others have shown no difference (8). However, overall the evidence seems to suggest that vitamin D3 is more effective at raising 25(OH) vitamin D levels than vitamin D2 (6). The source of vitamin D2 is always plant-based but vitamin D3 can be from animal or plant-based sources (9). Vitamin D3 is usually sourced from lanolin in sheep's wool but it can also be sourced from lichen (10).

7 DEHYDROCHOLESTEROL

LIVER

ACTIVE
FORM OF
VITAMIN D

KIDNEYS

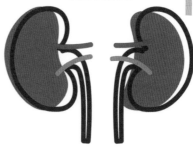

Can you take too much vitamin D?

Yes, vitamin D can be toxic in high amounts. It can also lead to high levels of calcium in the blood (hypercalcaemia) from increased absorption of calcium in the gut and the release of calcium stores from bones, which results in calcium being deposited in soft tissues (6). Too much sun exposure can't cause vitamin D toxicity though, as the body has a maximum level of pre-vitamin D3 in the skin that can be formed.

However, you can get too much vitamin D from supplements, so it's important not to take more than the recommended dose (6). The Expert Group on Vitamins and Minerals felt that a safe upper level for vitamin D could not be established based on the available research (11). A 'guidance level' for adults has been suggested of 25μg (micrograms) per day from supplements, not including vitamin D from foods (6, 11). In the US, the Institute of Medicine has established an upper level (UL) of 100μg of vitamin D per day for adults, 38μg/day for infants between six and 12 months of age, and 25μg per day for infants up to six months of age (12).

Plant-based diets and vitamin D

Very few foods naturally contain vitamin D, with fatty fish being the main source and to a lesser extent eggs. Many foods are fortified with vitamin D; in the United States it is common practice to fortify cow's milk with vitamin D whereas in the UK, some breakfast cereals and margarines are fortified with vitamin D (13). Mushrooms are a potential source of vitamin D2 if they have been exposed to UVB radiation, but the amount they contain varies widely and has been reported to be anywhere between 13 and 30μg per 100g (14, 15). The standard mushrooms that you can buy in the supermarket don't usually contain much vitamin D as they are grown in the dark (6).

How much vitamin D do children need?

Age	Safe intake (μg per day)
0-12 months	8.5-10*
1-3 years	10
4-6 years	10

*This is the safe intake as no DRV (dietary reference value) has been set for this age group.

In the UK, the government recommends a vitamin D supplement of 8.5-10µg per day (340-400IU) from birth for all breastfed babies. From six months to five years of age, a supplement of vitamins A and D is recommended unless they are drinking more than 500ml of infant formula per day, as these are already supplemented. These recommendations are for ALL children and not only children following a plant-based eating pattern. The daily recommended amounts are as follows:

Vitamin D: 10µg (400IU)

Vitamin A: 233µg RE (retinol equivalents)*

Until recently, 20mg of vitamin C was also recommended from six months to five years of age (16). However, the SACN 2023 report found that vitamin C intakes exceeded the reference nutrient intake across all age groups and therefore vitamin C supplementation is no longer recommended (17). The report also stated that there is no evidence that taking vitamin C supplements at the previous recommended level of 20mg per day has any adverse effects.

A lack of vitamin D causes a softening of the bones, known as rickets in children and osteomalacia in adults. Symptoms that you may experience include bone pain or aches, tiredness, muscle weakness or aches, and changes in mood or depression.

*1 RE is defined as 1µg of retinol (vitamin A) or 6µg of beta-carotene (see the next section on vitamin A for further details).

VITAMIN A

WHAT IS VITAMIN A AND WHY IS IT IMPORTANT?

Vitamin A is a fat-soluble vitamin, also known as retinol, which has a key role to play in keeping the immune system and our skin healthy as well as helping with vision, particularly in dim light (18). Good sources of vitamin A include oily fish, eggs, and full-fat versions of cow's milk, cheese and yoghurt. Liver and liver products are also extremely high in vitamin A; if you do include them in your eating pattern, only offer them once a week and avoid during pregnancy. You may have noticed that these are all animal-based sources! These foods all contain what we call 'pre-formed vitamin A' but plants are an excellent source of beta-carotene, which the body can convert into vitamin A (18).

CAN YOU HAVE TOO MUCH VITAMIN A?

Yes, if it is from animal-based sources you can consume too much vitamin A, as it is a fat-soluble vitamin and stored in the liver. If your vitamin A is coming from plant-based sources, then your body will only convert as much beta-carotene to vitamin A as it needs.

PLANT-BASED DIETS AND VITAMIN A

In two VeChi studies looking at children aged one to three years and six to 18 years in Germany, there was no difference in vitamin A intakes between the vegan, vegetarian and omnivore diet groups (2, 19). This illustrates that although vegan diets may contain no pre-formed vitamin A, they provide sufficient amounts of beta-carotene, which is converted to vitamin A in the body. Good plant-based food sources of beta-carotene include red, orange and yellow fruits and vegetables such as carrots, mango, papaya, apricots, bell peppers, sweet potatoes, and melon, as well as green leafy vegetables like kale and spinach.

How much vitamin A do children need?

Age	RNI* (μg per day)
0-12 months	350
1-3 years	400
4-6 years	400
Adults	600
Breastfeeding	350 in addition to the above

Symptoms of a vitamin A deficiency include dry eyes (called xerophthalmia), difficulty seeing in low light (night blindness) and increased susceptibility to infections.

* RNI = reference nutrient intake

WATER SOLUBLE VITAMINS

Water soluble vitamins are a diverse group of compounds that are essential to our health; deficiencies can result in a range of abnormalities from anaemia to growth failure and neurological disorders (20). They play a key role in many different processes in the body, such as the breakdown of protein, carbohydrates and fats at the cellular level. We need to obtain water-soluble vitamins from the foods that we eat as humans cannot produce them. Interestingly, while our diets undoubtedly provide the majority of these vitamins, there is more research accumulating that our gut bacteria play a significant role in providing some of these vitamins, particularly to the cells in our large intestine (21).

Water-soluble vitamins include B vitamins and vitamin C (also known as ascorbic acid). There are various B vitamins as follows: B1 (thiamin), B2 (riboflavin), B3 (niacin), B6 (pyridoxine), B12 (cobalamin), folate or folic acid, pantothenic acid, and biotin. I will be focusing on vitamins B12 and B2 in this section as they are less abundant in a plant-based eating pattern.

VITAMIN B12

What is vitamin B12 and why is it important?

Vitamin B12, also known as cobalamin, is one of the B vitamins that has a very important role in many different body processes. Vitamin B12 is involved in keeping our nervous system healthy, the formation of blood cells in the bone marrow, and DNA synthesis by activating folate, which is another B vitamin (22). So, you can see that vitamin B12 has a vital role to play in keeping our body healthy!

The symptoms of vitamin B12 deficiency can be divided into two broad categories: neurological (nerve-related) and haematological (blood-related). Symptoms involving the nerves may include pins and needles, vision problems, memory loss, loss of physical co-ordination (ataxia) and damage to the nerves in your hands and feet (peripheral neuropathy) (22). Symptoms involving the blood can include a type of anaemia where very large blood cells are formed (called megaloblastic anaemia) which is caused by impaired DNA synthesis. This type of anaemia causes symptoms including fatigue, irritability, decreased appetite, numbness or tingling in hands and feet, diarrhoea and weak muscles. These symptoms are very vague and may be caused by many other conditions, so please consult your child's doctor if you are concerned (23, 24).

Vitamin B12 deficiencies are diagnosed by a blood test that involves a number of biomarkers, as there is no one single biomarker for vitamin B12 deficiency. Vitamin B12 can be measured in the blood but levels of methylmalonic acid (MMA), homocysteine and holotranscobalamin (holoTC) are also measured, as together these biochemical measures give us a more accurate understanding about the vitamin B12 status and how it is working at the cellular level. Low serum vitamin B12 levels, combined with low holoTC and raised MMA and homocysteine levels, indicate a likely functional vitamin B12 deficiency (25, 26).

IMPORTANT:

Symptoms of a vitamin B12 deficiency can be extremely serious and sometimes irreversible. It is VITAL that anyone following a vegan diet is receiving adequate amounts of vitamin B12 through fortified foods and supplements. I cannot emphasise this enough.

Plant-based diets and vitamin B12 intakes in children

Vitamin B12 is only made by micro-organisms and is therefore not found in any plant foods, unless the food is contaminated with soil or has been fortified with vitamin B12 (23). The results of a VeChi study confirmed that vitamin B12 supplementation is essential in vegan diets (2, 19). The vegan group of children in this study had the lowest vitamin B12 intakes (without supplements) but the highest intakes with supplementation. 97% of children in the vegan group and 35% of children in the vegetarian group were taking vitamin B12 supplements; the vegetarian group of children also had a low intake of vitamin B12.

The VeChi Youth Study of six- to 18-year-olds found that when holoTC and MMA levels were taken into account, 13% of vegetarian children and 8% of vegan children were likely deficient in vitamin B12. The fact that fewer vegan children than vegetarian children were deficient in vitamin B12 is likely explained by the fact that more of the vegan group than the vegetarian group were taking vitamin B12 supplements (19). Based on their findings, both VeChi studies recommend that vitamin B12 supplementation should be encouraged for not only vegans but vegetarians too (2, 19). A recent review also recommended that vegetarians should supplement their diet with vitamin B12, and that screening for vitamin B12 deficiency should be encouraged (26).

Breastfed babies of vegan mums are at particular risk of developing vitamin B12 deficiency as breast milk levels of vitamin B12 are highly correlated to the vitamin B12 intake of breastfeeding women; therefore, they should be supported to ensure that they are receiving adequate levels of vitamin B12. An adequate vitamin B12 intake is also extremely important during pregnancy to ensure an adequate supply of vitamin B12 is delivered to the developing baby (27).

What are the best plant-based sources of vitamin B12?

Dairy alternative drinks, yoghurts and cheeses are often fortified with vitamin B12 but not always, so make sure you check the label. Nutritional yeast is another food product that is often fortified with vitamin B12 but not all brands are fortified, so always double check. Even if your child is eating foods fortified with vitamin B12, I still recommend a supplement to ensure an adequate and reliable source of vitamin B12, as toddlers' food intakes can be highly variable and unpredictable.

How much vitamin B12 do children need?

Age	RNI* (µg per day)	PBHP Recommended Daily Amounts (µg)
0-6 months	0.3	Breast milk or infant formula
7-12 months	0.4	2.5-5 (when eating 3 meals per day)
1-3 years	0.5	2.5-5
4-6 years	0.8	10-25
Breastfeeding	2.0	10-25

*RNI = Reference Nutrient Intake from foods
PBHP = Plant Based Health Professionals UK

Can children take too much vitamin B12?

There are no toxic upper limits for vitamin B12 that have been set by the Expert Group on Vitamins and Minerals in the UK, as there are insufficient data from studies on humans to establish a Safe Upper Level for vitamin B12 (11). Vitamin B12 is a water-soluble vitamin, so any amount taken in excess of requirements will be passed out in the urine. What this means in practical terms is that it does not matter very much if you or your child takes slightly more than the recommended amounts suggested in the table, although I wouldn't recommend mega-doses of any vitamin.

In a nutshell...

All children following a vegetarian and vegan diet should have a reliable source of vitamin B12, and the best way of ensuring this is to provide a supplement of at least 2.5-5µg each day.

VITAMIN B2

What is vitamin B2 and why is it important?

Vitamin B2, also known as riboflavin, is a water-soluble vitamin that we cannot make ourselves, so we need to obtain it from the foods that we eat. Riboflavin is involved in many bodily processes as it is a co-factor in a lot of enzyme reactions. It is involved in the repair of genetic material (DNA) and the production of energy, fats and amino acids (building blocks of protein) as well as activating folic acid (another B vitamin). Riboflavin is not stored in the body, so a regular daily supply is required from the foods that we eat (28).

A deficiency of vitamin B2 can cause quite vague or non-specific symptoms such as fatigue, a swollen throat, blurred vision and depression. It can also cause skin problems such as cracking skin, itching and dry skin around the mouth. Vitamin B2 deficiency doesn't usually occur in isolation; people who have a deficiency of vitamin B2 usually have a deficiency of other vitamins or nutrients too (29).

Plant-based diets and vitamin B2

The VeChi Youth Study found low blood levels of vitamin B2 in a significant proportion (>35%) of the study sample across all three diet groups (vegan, vegetarian and omnivorous). However, the vegan group of children had the lowest intake of vitamin B2 compared to the other two groups (19). In the VeChi study of one- to three-year-olds, the vegan group of children also had the lowest intakes of vitamin B2 (2) which highlights how important it is for all parents, but particularly those of vegan children, to make sure children have an adequate intake of vitamin B2.

Mushrooms, almonds and nutritional yeast are the best plant-based sources of vitamin B2. If you include dairy products in your child's eating pattern, they are another good source of vitamin B2. Many fortified dairy alternative drinks also contain vitamin B2 – always check the label.

A SUMMARY OF VITAMINS' FUNCTIONS AND FOOD SOURCES

Nutrient	Function	Food Sources
WATER-SOLUBLE VITAMINS		
Vitamin B1	Release energy from food Help nervous system and heart function properly	Breads, fortified breakfast cereals, nuts and seeds, beans and peas Meat, especially pork
Vitamin B2	Release energy from food Reduce tiredness Help to maintain normal skin and nervous system	Fortified breakfast cereals, mushrooms, almonds Offal, dairy products, eggs, some oily fish
Vitamin B3	Release energy from food Reduce tiredness Help to maintain normal skin and nervous system	Wholegrains (such as brown rice, wholewheat pasta, quinoa), bread, peanuts, sesame seeds Meat, poultry, fish, shellfish
Vitamin B6	Make red blood cells Help immune system work properly Regulate hormones Reduce tiredness	Fortified breakfast cereals, yeast extract, soya beans, sesame seeds, some fruit and vegetables including banana, avocado and green pepper Meat, poultry, fish, egg yolk
Vitamin B12*	Make red blood cells Help nervous system function properly Reduce tiredness	Fortified nutritional yeast, fortified breakfast cereals Meat, fish, shellfish, dairy products, eggs
Folate	Make red blood cells Reduce tiredness Help immune system work properly Development of the nervous system in unborn babies	Green leafy vegetables, some breads such as malted wheat and brown bread, peas and beans, oranges, berries, fortified breakfast cereals Offal
Vitamin C	Protect cells from damage Help form collagen, a connective tissue important for bones, teeth and skin Help immune system and nervous system function properly	Citrus fruit, blackcurrants, strawberries, papaya, kiwi fruit, broccoli, brussels sprouts, bell peppers, potatoes, tomatoes
FAT-SOLUBLE VITAMINS		
Vitamin A	Help the immune system function properly Help with vision Maintenance of normal skin	Dark green leafy vegetables, orange-coloured fruits and vegetables (e.g. carrot, sweet potato, butternut squash, cantaloupe melon, papaya) Liver, cheese, eggs
Vitamin D*	Help with calcium absorption Maintain healthy bones and muscles Involved in the immune system	Fortified breakfast cereals, fat spreads Oily fish, eggs
Vitamin E	Protect cells from damage	Vegetable and seed oils (e.g. olive, rapeseed, sunflower, peanut), almonds, sunflower seeds, avocados, olives
Vitamin K	Help with blood clotting Required for normal bone structure	Leafy greens, broccoli, green beans, peas, rapeseed oil, olive oil, soya oil

*Indicates recommended supplements: see the table on page 94 in Chapter 4.

Source: 30

NUTRITIOUS* AND
PACKED WITH PROTEIN

NO SUGARS
SOYA

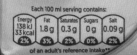
NO SUGARS

Each 100 ml serving contains:

Energy 138 kJ 33 kcal 2%	Fat 1.8 g 3%	Saturates 0.3 g 2%	Sugars 0 g 0%	Salt 0.09 g 2%

of an adult's reference intake**

PLANT-BASED
WITH CALCIUM

Carbon Neutral   Organic   High in Protein

Cauldron™

Quick & Tasty
TOFU

Ready to cook
tofu block

Scan for
tofu tips

250g℮
Recipe suggestion

RICH IN PROTEIN. LOW IN FAT

NO SUGARS
PLAIN

MADE FROM SOYA

PLANT-BASED
WITH LIVE CULTURES

Energy 179 kJ 43 kcal 2%	Fat 2.3 g 3%	Saturates 0.4 g 2%

of an adult's reference

MINERALS AND TRACE ELEMENTS

Minerals and trace elements are micronutrients (along with vitamins) that are needed in small quantities by the body, usually in milligram quantities. Examples of minerals include calcium, iron and magnesium. Trace elements (or trace metals) are micronutrients needed in tiny quantities by the body, usually microgram quantities, such as iodine, selenium and copper. Below, I'll cover minerals and trace elements that are particularly important to all babies and young children, with special reference to plant-based sources and what the literature tells us about the intakes of these minerals in plant-based children.

CALCIUM

WHAT IS CALCIUM AND WHY IS IT IMPORTANT FOR CHILDREN?

The human body cannot make its own calcium, so we need to obtain it from the foods we eat. Calcium is a very important mineral for the formation of bones and teeth. It's the most abundant mineral in the body, with 99% of calcium being stored in bones and teeth, and just 1% in the blood (31). As well as being an important structural component of the skeleton, calcium is also important for muscle contractions and normal blood clotting in the body.

An adequate calcium intake in childhood is one of the important nutritional factors for acquiring peak bone mineral density in early adulthood. It is important to ensure that a high peak bone mineral density (PBM) is acquired, as PBM starts to decrease after this. A low calcium intake in childhood may lead to low bone mineral density and subsequently an increased risk of osteoporosis later in life (32).

Blood levels of calcium are very closely controlled within a narrow range by mechanisms involving the kidneys, the bone and the gastrointestinal tract (31). Measuring blood levels of calcium does not tell us anything about the overall body stores of calcium or the bone mineral density. Instead of a blood test, a scan called a dual energy x-ray absorptiometry (DEXA) is used to measure bone mineral density and body composition (33).

ARE CALCIUM INTAKES A PROBLEM IN PLANT-BASED CHILDREN?

Potentially, they can be. In the VeChi study of one- to three-year-old children, vegan children had the lowest calcium intakes of the three diet groups, with the average calcium intakes being 320mg per day in the vegan group, 399mg per day in the vegetarian group, and 445mg per day in the omnivorous group (2). The recommended calcium intake in the UK is 350mg per day for one- to three-year-olds and 450mg per day for four- to six-year-olds.

In contrast, the National Diet and Nutrition Survey (NDNS) data from the UK showed that calcium intakes in young children were more than double the reference nutrient intake (RNI), at 718mg per day on average for one- to three-year-olds (34). This data was from children who were including dairy products in their diets.

In the VeChi Youth Study of six- to 18-year-olds, the vegan group also had the lowest calcium intake, but all three diet groups had calcium intakes below the reference value (19). Vegan participants had average daily calcium intakes of 305mg, vegetarians 390mg and the omnivorous group 400mg.

Another study of five- to ten-year-old Polish children found that the vegetarian and vegan groups had lower bone mineral content (BMC) than the omnivorous group, although the lower BMC was no longer present when adjustments were made for a smaller body size in the vegetarian group (35). However, the vegan group still showed the lowest BMC even when adjustments were made for their lower body size. What this study didn't report was data on the calcium and vitamin D intakes of the children, which would have been important to look at to see if the vegan group of children had lower calcium and vitamin D intakes than the other groups.

The key message from these studies is that we must ensure that vegan and plant-based children have adequate calcium intakes, as well as other ways to support bone health, such as adequate vitamin D and protein intakes as well as weight-bearing exercise.

CAN CHILDREN GET ENOUGH CALCIUM WITHOUT DAIRY?

In short, yes they can! But that doesn't mean we shouldn't pay attention to the calcium intake of plant-based children: quite the opposite, in fact. The studies mentioned above showed us that vegan children can have low intakes of calcium, so we must ensure that plant-based children have an adequate calcium intake. But this does not necessarily have to be from dairy products.

Dairy products are an excellent source of calcium, protein, fats (in full-fat versions), iodine and vitamins B2 and B12. It is these nutrients that are essential, not the dairy products themselves. So, we need to ensure that plant-based children are getting enough of these essential nutrients from other sources. One of the best ways to provide enough calcium to plant-based children is to offer a fortified dairy alternative drink, such as fortified soya milk as a snack and with porridge or cereal in the morning.

The table below illustrates some of the best plant-based sources of calcium for children. Take note of the portion sizes as I have aimed to illustrate typical and realistic amounts that toddlers would eat and drink. See Chapter 6 for more information and details about what types of plant-based dairy alternative drinks I recommend and why.

Food	Portion Size	Calcium (mg)
Breast milk	100ml	30-40mg
Cow's milk	100ml	120mg
Yoghurt	45g (3 tbsp)	60mg
Cheddar-type cheese	15g	120mg
Fortified soya/pea/oat drink	100ml	120mg
Fortified dairy alternative yoghurts	45g (3 tbsp)	50-60mg
Fortified dairy alternative cheddar-type cheese e.g. Koko*	15g	120mg
Fortified breads e.g. Kingsmill 50/50 Vitamin Boost, Hovis Best of Both	½-1 slice	134-150mg (per slice)
Broccoli, boiled	1 floret (45g)	20mg
Kale, boiled	20g	30mg
Okra, boiled	25g	30mg
Pak choi	30g	30mg
Sesame seeds	1 tsp (4g)	27mg
Tahini	1 tsp (6g)	40mg
Almonds, finely ground	1 tbsp (7g)	17mg
Calcium-set tofu	45g	180mg
Magnesium-set tofu	45g	65mg
Fortified oat cereals e.g. Ready Oats	18g	240mg

*Note that many plant-based cheeses are NOT fortified with calcium, so always check the label.

How much calcium do children need?

AGE	RNI* (MG PER DAY)
0-12 months	525mg
1-3 years	350mg
4-6 years	450mg
Breastfeeding	1250mg

Peak bone density is reached in early adulthood (typically in your twenties) so it is important to ensure an adequate calcium intake throughout childhood and adolescence in order to reach a maximum bone density (32).

*RNI = Reference Nutrient Intake from foods

Calcium bioavailability

Calcium bioavailability is the degree to which calcium can be absorbed, used by the body and incorporated into bone (32). Vitamin D has a positive effect on calcium absorption, as it improves the absorption of calcium from the gut.

There are many plants that contain significant amounts of calcium but the presence of various components within plants (such as oxalic and phytic acid) can decrease the absorption or bioavailability of calcium from plants. Oxalic acid is also known as oxolate and phytic acid is also known as phytate. Generally, the amount of calcium absorbed from dairy products is around 30% (32).

Spinach is an example of a vegetable with a high amount of calcium, but because spinach also contains a high amount of oxalates, only around 5% of the calcium in spinach is absorbed. However, many other green vegetables are low in oxalates and therefore excellent sources of highly bioavailable calcium (around 50% of calcium absorbed). Examples of low oxalate and high calcium vegetables include broccoli, kale, pak choi, watercress, spring greens, and sweet potatoes (32).

Soya beans and products made with soya, such as soya milk, appear to be an exception in that soya beans contain significant amounts of phytic and oxalic acids, but the absorption of calcium from fortified soya drinks is very good (around 30-40%). This was confirmed in a study about the absorption of calcium from fortified dairy alternative soya drinks which was reported to be equivalent to cow's milk (37). Remember to shake the carton of fortified dairy alternative drink though, as the added calcium can settle to the bottom due to poor solubility (32).

Calcium Absorbability	Plant-Based Food Source
Good (around 30-50%)	Fortified plant-based dairy alternative drinks, calcium-set tofu (e.g. Cauldron brand), low-oxalate vegetables such as kale, broccoli, brussels sprouts, pak choi, watercress, spring greens, calcium-containing mineral water
Fair (around 20%)	Pinto beans, red beans, white beans
Poor (around 10% or less)	Sesame seeds, rhubarb
Very poor (around 5%)	Spinach

Sources: 31, 36

IRON

WHAT IS IRON AND WHY IS IT SO IMPORTANT FOR CHILDREN?

Iron is a critical nutrient for babies and young children and iron deficiency is the most common nutrient deficiency in the world, regardless of dietary pattern (37). Iron is a mineral that is needed for the formation of haemoglobin in red blood cells, which transports oxygen around the body, and for myoglobin in muscle cells, where oxygen is stored and used by the muscles (38). Iron is also needed for the proper functioning of many enzymes in the body, particularly those involved in the functioning of the nerves and brain. Iron is therefore vital for the developing brain and prolonged iron deficiency anaemia, especially during the time of rapid brain growth, can result in cognitive (learning) and motor (movement) delays in children. So, it is extremely important to ensure that babies and young children are offered iron-rich foods at each meal from six months of age (39).

The reason that iron is considered a critical nutrient for babies is that babies are born with enough iron stores to last approximately six months (if they were born at full term and were a good birth weight). After six months of age, iron levels start to decrease so an additional source of iron from foods needs to be added to a baby's nutritional intake. Breast milk contains a tiny amount of iron and after the age of six months, this isn't enough to keep up with your baby's growth. Iron is the main nutritional reason for starting babies on solids at around six months of age and it is a priority nutrient when considering which foods to offer to babies (40).

Data from the most recent National Diet and Nutrition Survey (NDNS) in the UK, which looks at the nutritional intake of a sample of children and adults from around the country, including children eating meat, found that the average iron intake of children aged 18 months to three years of age was 5.8mg per day. 11% of the sample had intakes that were considered 'very low' as they fell below 3.7mg per day (41, 42).

Factors that increase the risk of iron deficiency include:

Premature birth (born before 36 weeks gestation)

Drinking too much cow's milk or fortified dairy alternative (more than 500-600ml a day for toddlers)

Low birth weight (less than 2.5kg)

Delayed introduction of solids (beyond seven months of age) or delayed introduction of iron-rich foods

ARE PLANT-BASED CHILDREN MORE LIKELY TO DEVELOP IRON DEFICIENCY ANAEMIA?

The short answer is no, but let me explain in a bit more detail for you. Studies on iron intakes in vegetarian and vegan children consistently show that iron intakes are higher in these groups than in omnivorous children. However, studies on iron status vary significantly in their results. Some studies (38) have found a higher amount of iron deficiency in vegan children, but other studies (43) have found no differences between vegan and omnivorous children in terms of serum ferritin levels, which is the marker for iron storage within the body. Our body uses up our iron stores first before haemoglobin levels start decreasing, so a low level of ferritin indicates early stage iron deficiency.

Iron status refers to the amount of iron within the body that can be used for various processes. In other words, iron status tells us whether a person has too little, just enough or too much iron within the body to meet their needs (38). There are several markers within the blood that can be used to assess the amount of iron stores within the body. For example, we can look at blood levels of ferritin (iron storage protein), haemoglobin, transferrin, iron, transferrin saturation, iron binding capacity, and haematocrit (44). Each of these blood markers can tell us slightly different information about iron within the body.

A study on iron status and dietary intake in vegetarian adults showed that the vegetarian and vegan groups had decreased iron stores (illustrated by lower ferritin levels and increased transferrin levels) compared to the omnivorous group (45). However, the vegetarian women also had decreased levels of a protein called hepcidin, which indicates that this group absorbed more iron in the gut. Hepcidin is a hormone that regulates how much iron is absorbed by the body so that there is enough for essential functions but not so much that cells experience iron overload (46). The results suggest that an adaptation occurred in this group, allowing the vegetarian women to absorb more iron. This was a small study and only related to adults, so we need to be cautious in interpreting the results. However, they could explain why vegetarians don't seem to have higher levels of iron deficiency anaemia, as the body seems to adapt to the situation.

IN A NUTSHELL...

Research on the iron status of vegetarian and vegan children is varied and inconsistent, but in general most of it shows that vegetarian children tend to have higher intakes of iron and lower iron stores but don't have higher rates of iron deficiency anaemia than omnivorous children.

Iron bioavailability

There are two types of iron within foods: haem iron and non-haem iron. Haem iron is found almost exclusively in animal foods (meats, organ meats, poultry, and seafood). Non-haem iron is found in meat and plant foods, with the richest sources of non-haem iron being cereals, vegetables, nuts, and eggs (38). Iron is also added to many foods and in the UK, it is mandatory to add iron to bread and wheat flour (38). Many breakfast cereals are also fortified with iron, although this is voluntary.

Around 20-30% of haem iron is absorbed from foods, compared to 5-15% of non-haem iron (38, 47). There are certain substances within plant foods that can make it more difficult to absorb iron from them, called iron inhibitors, which include phytate, polyphenols and calcium. Phytates are found in seeds, nuts, beans, lentils, and wholegrains (particularly wheat bran). Polyphenols are found in tea, coffee, red wine, dark chocolate, and spinach – so not particularly relevant to young children! Calcium, which of course is found in most dairy products and fortified dairy alternatives, has been shown to decrease the absorption of both types of iron (haem and non-haem).

Don't worry too much about these compounds though, as soaking, cooking, sprouting, and fermenting all decrease the phytate content of foods, so beans, lentils, nuts, and seeds can still provide fantastic sources of iron. I don't recommend tea or coffee as a drink for toddlers, but if your child was to have one of these drinks, it should be offered between meals so as not to decrease their absorption of iron from food. For calcium-rich foods such as cow's milk, other dairy products and fortified dairy alternatives, avoid offering large amounts of these and aim to offer calcium-rich drinks between meals. Balance is important; remember we want the overall calcium intake to be enough to support your little one's bone health but not so much as to decrease the absorption of iron-rich foods. I'll be talking about this in more detail throughout Chapter 6.

You may be wondering if there is anything you can do about this decreased absorption of iron. The good news is yes, you can! As well as iron inhibitors, there are also substances that increase the absorption of iron, called iron enhancers, and plant foods are excellent sources of these. Some examples of iron enhancers include vitamin C (broccoli, strawberries, potatoes, citrus fruits, kiwi fruit, tomatoes, brussels sprouts, and peppers are particularly good sources) and beta-carotene (carrots, mango, papaya, apricots, sweet potatoes, pumpkin, butternut squash, melon, and red/orange/yellow peppers) as well as onions and garlic (48, 49, 50).

How much iron do children need?

Age	RNI* (mg per day)
0-3 months	1.7
4-6 months	4.3
7-12 months	7.8
1-3 years	6.9
4-6 years	6.1

*RNI = Reference Nutrient Intake from foods

Pale skin or lighter skin than the rest of the family, tiredness and lack of energy, shortness of breath, heart palpitations, and poor appetite (especially in babies and young children) can all be symptoms of iron deficiency (51). There are reasons other than our diet that can cause iron deficiency anaemia, but many of these are more common in adults. Some underlying medical reasons include menstruation (particularly if periods are heavy), undiagnosed coeliac disease, pregnancy, blood loss from gastrointestinal disorders, and bleeding ulcers but this is not an exhaustive list. Please discuss with your GP if you are concerned about yourself or your child.

HOW CAN I MAKE SURE MY PLANT-BASED EATER IS GETTING ENOUGH IRON?

Don't worry, you don't have to count the milligrams of iron your child is eating each day! I recommend offering an iron-rich food at every meal (three times per day) alongside foods that are rich in vitamin C and beta-carotene to maximise the absorption of iron. Onions and garlic also improve the absorption of iron, so aim to include these in some meals too if you can. By regularly offering iron-rich foods alongside foods that increase the absorption of iron, as well as limiting the total amount of calcium-rich foods offered, you are giving your child the best possible opportunity to obtain sufficient iron from their foods. Check out Chapter 7 on meal planning where I will be going into this in more detail and giving you plenty of practical examples of how you can put meals together that maximise nutrition for your little one.

Good Sources of Plant-Based Iron

Food	Iron (mg) per 100g	Typical toddler portion size	Iron per portion (mg)
LEGUMES (COOKED)			
Red lentils	2.3mg	3 tbsp	1mg
Green lentils	3.5mg	3 tbsp	1.3mg
Puy lentils	3.5mg	3 tbsp	1.3mg
Chickpeas	1.5-2.1mg	3 tbsp	0.6-0.8mg
Black beans	2.1mg	3 tbsp	1mg
Butter beans	1.5mg	3 tbsp	0.7mg
Peas	1.8mg	1 tbsp	0.5mg
Falafel	3.4mg	2 mini falafels (25g each)	1.7mg
Hummus	1.9mg	1-2 tbsp	0.6-1.2mg
Tofu	3.5mg	50-100g	1.6-3.5mg
FORTIFIED CEREALS AND BREADS			
Fortified wheat-based cereals e.g. Weetabix	11.9mg	1 Weetabix (20g)	2.2mg
Fortified oat-based cereals e.g. Ready Oats	12mg	20g	2.4mg
GRAINS (UNCOOKED)			
Oat flakes, rolled	3.6mg	3 tbsp (30g)	1.1mg
Quinoa	7.8mg	3 tbsp (30g)	2.3mg
Pasta	1.8mg	3 tbsp (30g)	0.5mg
Lentil pasta	7.6mg	3 tbsp (30g)	2.3mg
GREEN LEAFY VEGETABLES			
Broccoli, steamed	0.6mg	1 floret (45g)	0.3mg
Spinach, boiled	1.6mg	1 tbsp (30g)	0.5mg

Note that the portion sizes are suggested for toddlers (aged one to four years) and are based on the midpoint between these ages. Please don't worry if your child eats more or less than the suggested amount on any given day; allow your child to eat according to their appetite.

IODINE

Iodine is not a very well-known micronutrient and often forgotten about, but we need to raise awareness about it, as iodine deficiency is common. Iodine is only needed in tiny microgram quantities, but it is vitally important for the proper functioning of the human body, especially your baby's growing and developing brain.

WHAT IS IODINE AND WHY IS IT IMPORTANT FOR CHILDREN?

Iodine is a mineral that is essential for the formation of thyroid hormones called thyroxine (T4) and triiodothyronine (T3). The thyroid is a gland found in the neck and thyroid hormones are needed for children's growth, regulating metabolism (how our body uses food for energy and growth) and for the development of a baby's brain during gestation and early life. Iodine is particularly important during gestation and for the first three years of a child's life. The thyroid is sensitive to both high and low levels of iodine, so we need to make sure that children are getting enough iodine but also that they are not having too much, as both can be harmful (52). It's a Goldilocks porridge situation, where we need to make sure that the amount of iodine that children are getting is 'just right'!

If your body does not have enough iodine, the thyroid gland starts to swell and enlarge as it attempts to obtain more iodine for thyroid hormone production. The thyroid gland swelling is called a goitre. Other consequences of iodine deficiency include growth impairment, problems with reproduction, and problems with the brain and cognition (53). I know some of these possible consequences of iodine deficiency sound scary, but that's why it is so important to make sure that children (and breastfeeding adults) are receiving enough iodine to protect their health and wellbeing.

ARE CHILDREN EATING PLANT–BASED DIETS AT RISK OF IODINE DEFICIENCY?

Yes, unfortunately they are. Those following a vegan diet have been recognised to be at increased risk of an iodine deficiency and vegetarians may also be at risk, depending on the amount of cow's milk and dairy products they include in their eating pattern (54).

The VeChi study found that vegan children had the lowest iodine intake, but all three diet groups (vegans, vegetarians and omnivores) had low iodine intakes that were below the recommended daily amount (20). Low iodine intakes of adults and children have also been reported in many other studies within Europe, so it is a widespread problem across all eating patterns (55). In the UK, there is no mandatory programme for iodising salt, as there is in many other countries around the world. Therefore, iodised salt is not readily available in the UK, unlike other areas of the world.

National dietary surveys have reported that milk and milk products provide almost two thirds (62%) of the iodine intakes of toddlers aged one and a half to three years and just over half (51%) of iodine intakes of four- to ten-year-old children (56). This illustrates how important it is to consider your child's iodine intake, especially if they do not include cow's milk and milk products in their usual eating pattern. Some dairy alternative drinks and yoghurts are now fortified with iodine but this is very variable between brands, so it is important to check the label. Please be aware that if the dairy alternative drink is organic, it will likely not be fortified with any vitamins or minerals.

Some dairy alternative drinks that do include iodine (as well as calcium and vitamins) include the following (this is not an exhaustive list and always check the label as products may change):

Tesco own brand dairy alternative drinks

ASDA own brand dairy alternative drinks

All Marks and Spencer dairy alternative drinks

Alpro Soya/Oat Growing Up Drink (the oat drink contains much less iodine than the soya drink)

Oatly oat drinks

MOMA oat drinks

MIGHTY oat- and pea-based drinks

WHAT ARE THE BEST FOOD SOURCES OF IODINE?

The best food sources of iodine in the UK are dairy products, eggs, white fish (oily fish contain much less iodine) and seafood. Plant foods are generally poor sources of iodine and the amount of iodine in plants varies widely due to variable quantities of iodine in the soil in which plants are grown. Cow's milk is naturally quite low in iodine but due to various farming practices, cow's milk ends up being a very good source of iodine because both their feed and some disinfectants used during milking contain iodine. The amount of iodine in cow's milk can also vary depending on the time of year; it generally contains more iodine in the winter months than in the summer months (57, 58).

Seaweed also contains significant amounts of iodine, but these are highly variable and can be excessive, so I generally don't recommend seaweed as a reliable source of iodine for children or for those who are breastfeeding. Nori seaweed has been found to contain the least iodine, while wakame, kombu and kelp types contain more iodine in varying amounts. For example, one small pack (5g) of Itsu Crispy Seaweed Thins contains 92-122μg (micrograms) of iodine, while an 18g bag of Abakus Foods Seaweed Crisps contains 32.3μg of iodine. Kombu seaweed can contain excessive amounts of iodine that can easily exceed the upper limit and I wouldn't recommend it for children or for anyone pregnant and breastfeeding (59).

HOW MUCH IODINE DO CHILDREN NEED?

AGE	RNI* (μG PER DAY)	WHO RECOMMENDATIONS (μG)
0-3 months	50	90
4-12 months	60	90
1-3 years	70	90
4-6 years	100	90
Adult females	140	150
Breastfeeding	140	250

*RNI = Reference Nutrient Intake from foods

The World Health Organisation (WHO) recommends an increase in iodine intake during pregnancy (not shown in the table) and breastfeeding, while UK recommendations do not reflect any increase from adult females to those breastfeeding (or pregnant), as it is assumed that adult women have sufficient iodine stores to last throughout their pregnancy and breastfeeding (56).

Good Sources of Iodine

Food	Portion Size	Iodine (μG)
Cow's milk*	100ml	25-50
Yoghurt	75g	25-50
Fortified dairy alternative drink**	100ml	13-30 (depending on brand)
Eggs	1 egg (50g)	25
Cod	60g	115
Haddock	60g	195
Salmon	50g	7
Tinned tuna	50g	6
Prawns	30g	3
Scampi	85g	80

*The iodine content of cow's milk depends on the season: lower in summer, higher in winter.

**Many dairy alternative drinks are not fortified with iodine; always check the label.

Sources: 57, 58

How can I make sure my little one is getting enough iodine?

If your family includes milk and dairy products daily and fish or seafood at least once a week in their eating pattern, then it is likely your little one will be receiving enough iodine from these foods. If your family is mostly or 100% plant-based, then I'd recommend an iodine supplement. You can also use fortified foods or drinks, such as dairy alternative drinks, as some of these are now fortified with iodine, but check the label to be sure.

Babies will receive all their iodine from their mother's breast milk (if the mother is eating adequate amounts of iodine-rich foods or taking an iodine supplement) or infant formula for the first six months of life. Once weaning foods have been established and breast milk or infant formula naturally decreases (from around 10-12 months of age), a supplement will likely be needed.

Feeling unsure about what supplements to give your little one? Or what supplements to take yourself if you are breastfeeding? Don't worry, I can help! I have included a very easy-to-follow table to help you work out what supplements you and your child need on page 94 of this book.

ZINC

What is zinc and why is it important for children?

Zinc is an essential mineral that has many important roles within the body, and is a co-factor (or 'helper') of enzymes involved in hundreds of chemical reactions in the body (60). Zinc is involved in processes including the growth of cells, the formation of DNA, building proteins, and healing damaged skin. It is also important for the proper functioning of the immune system, wound healing, our taste and smell, and children's growth, as zinc helps cells to grow and multiply. This means that a good zinc intake is particularly important during times of rapid growth, such as early childhood, adolescence and pregnancy (61).

Sources of zinc in food

Both animal and plant foods contain good amounts of zinc. However, like iron, zinc from animal foods is better absorbed than zinc found in plant foods. The best animal-based sources of zinc include oysters, shellfish, fish, beef, poultry, pork, and dairy products. The best plant-based sources of zinc include nuts, seeds, legumes (such as lentils and beans), wholegrains, cereals, nutritional yeast, and mycoprotein, which is what Quorn® products are made of. See the table on page 79 for more detail about these sources of zinc.

Zinc bioavailability

Bioavailability means the amount of a nutrient that is absorbed in the gut and available to be used by the body. Although there are plenty of sources of zinc in plant-based foods, the bioavailability or absorption of zinc from these foods is lower than from animal-based sources, due to certain substances present within plants called phytates. These are known as 'anti-nutrients' and can decrease the amounts of zinc (and iron, as mentioned earlier in this chapter) that our bodies can absorb from plant foods. Phytate, or phytic acid, is the main form of storage for phosphorus within cereals, legumes (beans and lentils), pulses, nuts and seeds. Phytates can form insoluble complexes with zinc and iron within the gut and therefore decrease the absorption of these minerals. Humans don't have the necessary enzyme, called phytase, to break down these insoluble complexes but bacteria do. This means that fermented foods are lower in phytates and therefore we can absorb more zinc from these foods.

Onions and garlic both increase the absorption of zinc too, and other ways to increase zinc's absorbability include soaking, cooking and sprouting plant foods to decrease their phytate content. Tinned beans, for example, already contain less phytates as they have been cooked at a high temperature and under pressure. Watch out for the salt content of tinned beans though and rinse thoroughly if they do contain salt. Those labelled 'in water' generally contain 0.03g of salt per 100g, compared to those 'in salted water' which contain 0.45g of salt per 100g.

DO VEGANS AND VEGETARIANS HAVE LOW ZINC STATUS?

Studies looking at zinc intakes and zinc status (the amount of zinc measured in the body) have variable results, with most finding no difference in zinc intake and zinc blood levels between vegetarian and non-vegetarian groups (62). Young children are at greater risk of zinc deficiency as they have high zinc requirements during times of rapid growth (63). So, it is important to provide plenty of zinc-rich foods in children's diets regardless of their eating pattern, such as ground nuts or nut butters, ground seeds or seed butters, legumes, and wholegrains. Nutritional yeast and mycoprotein products such as Quorn® are particularly good sources of zinc.

WHAT ARE THE SIGNS OF A ZINC DEFICIENCY?

Zinc deficiency is difficult to detect as there is a lack of reliable blood tests to accurately identify zinc status. Currently, the best way to check zinc status is to look at the levels of zinc in the blood (63-65). Symptoms of a zinc deficiency could include impaired wound healing, decreased sense of taste or smell, impaired immune function or increased risk of infections, slowing down of children's growth, and impaired cognitive function (learning and memory).

HOW MUCH ZINC DO CHILDREN NEED?

AGE	RNI* (MG PER DAY)
0-6 months	4mg
7-12 months	5mg
1-3 years	5mg
4-6 years	6.5mg
Adult females	7mg
Breastfeeding	+6mg (0-4 months) +2.5mg (4+ months) In addition to RNI for adult females (above)

*RNI = Reference Nutrient Intake from foods

Good plant-based sources of zinc

Food	Portion size	Zinc (mg)
SEEDS		
Hemp seeds	10g (1 tbsp)	1mg
Pumpkin seeds	10g (1 tbsp)	0.67mg
Chia seeds	10g (1 tbsp)	0.5mg
Linseeds (flaxseed)	10g (1 tbsp)	0.4mg
NUTS*		
Cashew nuts	15g (2 tbsp)	0.9mg
Walnuts	15g (2 tbsp)	0.4mg
Almonds	15g (2 tbsp)	0.5mg
Brazil nuts	15g (2 tbsp)	0.7mg
LEGUMES		
Red lentils, cooked	40g	0.4mg
Chickpeas, tinned	40g	0.3mg
Red kidney beans, cooked	40g	0.3mg
Tofu	50g	0.8mg
Peanuts*	15g (2 tbsp)	0.5mg
WHOLEGRAINS		
Wholemeal bread	1 slice	0.6mg
Quinoa, cooked	75g	0.8mg
OTHER		
Nutritional yeast	5g (1 tbsp)	6mg
Quorn® (mycoprotein)	75g	5.7mg
DAIRY PRODUCTS		
Full-fat cow's milk	100ml	0.4mg
Full-fat plain yoghurt	60g (1 small pot)	0.4mg

*Do not offer whole nuts or large seeds to young children; use ground nuts/seeds or smooth nut/seed butters.
Sources: 66, 67

A SUMMARY OF MINERALS' FUNCTIONS AND FOOD SOURCES

Nutrient	Function	Food Source
Calcium	Build and maintain strong bones and teeth Help with blood clotting Help nerves and muscles to function properly	Fortified dairy alternatives, bread (white, brown, wholegrain), leafy green vegetables such as broccoli, kale, watercress, pak choi Dairy products, canned fish with soft bones
Iodine*	Help to make thyroid hormones Help the brain to function normally	Some fortified dairy alternatives, seaweed** Dairy products, white fish, shellfish, eggs
Iron	Make red blood cells Help the immune system to function properly Involved in the functioning of the brain and learning	Beans, pulses, nuts, seeds, quinoa, wholemeal bread, dried fruit, fortified breakfast cereals Offal, red meat, oily fish
Magnesium	Release energy from food Maintain strong bones Help nerves and muscles to function properly	Brazil nuts, sunflower seeds, wholegrain breakfast cereals, wholegrain and seeded breads, brown rice, quinoa
Zinc	Maintain healthy hair, nails and skin Help with wound healing Contribute to fertility and reproduction Contribute to normal mental skills	Pumpkin seeds, pine nuts, wholegrain breakfast cereals, wholegrain and seeded breads Meat, poultry, cheese, crab, mussels, cockles
Selenium	Protect cells from damage Help the immune system to function properly Maintain normal skin and nails Help fertility in males	Brazil nuts, cashew nuts, sunflower seeds Eggs, offal, poultry, fish, shellfish
Copper	Help to produce red and white blood cells Involved in iron metabolism Formation of collagen (part of connective tissue and bones)	Tree nuts, peanuts, seeds Shellfish, offal
Fluoride	Help form strong bones and teeth to reduce the risk of tooth decay	Tap water, toothpaste
Manganese	Co-factor for many enzymes Protect cells from damage Involved in bone formation, reproduction, blood clotting Help the immune system to function properly	Tree nuts, wholegrain cereals, seeds, legumes, leafy greens, spices such as black pepper Mussels, oysters, clams

*An iodine supplement is likely needed; please see the table on page 94.

**Seaweed can contain excessive quantities of iodine so is not recommended for children or those who are pregnant or breastfeeding.

Sources: 30, 68, 69

A SUMMARY OF MINERALS' FUNCTIONS AND FOOD SOURCES

Nutrient	Function	Food Source
Molybdenum	Co-factor for many enzymes Involved in the metabolism of sulphur-containing amino acids and DNA (genetic material) Help break down certain drugs and toxic substances	Found in a wide variety of foods including legumes, wholegrain cereals, tree nuts, rice, potatoes, bananas, leafy greens Dairy products, beef, chicken, eggs
Sodium	Help regulate the water balance in the body	Very small amounts found naturally in foods. Most sodium comes from added salt (sodium chloride) during processing, preparation, preserving and serving of foods.
Magnesium	Release energy from food Maintain strong bones Help nerves and muscles to function properly	Brazil nuts, sunflower seeds, wholegrain breakfast cereals, wholegrain and seeded breads, brown rice, quinoa
Potassium	Help regulate the water balance in the body Maintain normal blood pressure Help nerves and muscles to function normally	Many fruits and vegetables such as bananas, blackcurrants, avocado, spinach, parsnip, and beetroot. Dried fruits such as apricots, sultanas and figs. Wholegrain breakfast cereals. Poultry, red meat, fish, cow's milk
Phosphorus	Build strong teeth and bones Help release energy from foods	Bread, wholegrains such as brown rice and wholewheat pasta Red meat, poultry, fish, dairy products, eggs
Chromium	Help the body to use carbohydrates, proteins and fats Help activate insulin receptors	Found in a wide variety of foods including wholegrain cereals, tree nuts, fruits and vegetables. Amounts vary depending on soil conditions. Meat
Chloride	Help balance electrolytes and fluids in the body Help maintain pH levels in the blood Production of hydrochloric acid (stomach acid needed for digestion)	Table salt as sodium chloride, seaweed, rye, tomatoes, lettuce, celery, olives Processed meats, small amounts in dairy products and non-processed meat

*An iodine supplement is likely needed; please see the table on page 94.

**Seaweed can contain excessive quantities of iodine so is not recommended for children or those who are pregnant or breastfeeding.

Sources: 30, 68, 69

CHAPTER 4
Plant Powered Tinies

Chapter 4
Plant Powered Tinies

FEEDING YOUR BABY
FROM BIRTH TO AROUND SIX MONTHS OF AGE

In this chapter I am going to be talking about feeding your baby in those early few months. It can be an incredibly overwhelming time, especially with your first baby. I remember feeling very anxious and overwhelmed by the experience as it is such a huge change to your life, physically, emotionally, and psychologically. But it is also incredibly rewarding and humbling. I found that having a group of friends around me (my National Childbirth Trust antenatal group) who were going through the same thing was an enormous help and source of support, especially as I don't have any family in the UK. I am still in touch with most of my NCT friends almost 17 years later!

BREASTFEEDING

Breastfeeding is the ideal way to feed your baby and the World Health Organisation (WHO) recommends exclusive breastfeeding for around six months, followed by continued breastfeeding until your child is at least two years old, alongside the introduction of appropriate foods including those rich in iron (1). Any amount of breast milk is beneficial for your baby, so don't worry if you are not able to breastfeed your baby exclusively.

There are many benefits of breastfeeding for both baby and mum. Human breast milk is a living substance that is actively changing and adapting to meet the needs of your baby as they grow (2). It really is incredible stuff! Breast milk contains antibodies (proteins that are produced by the immune system in response to the presence of bacteria or viruses) that are passed to your baby to help protect them from various infections. This explains one of the benefits of breastfeeding for your baby, which is a decreased risk of infections, particularly ear, chest and gastrointestinal (gut) infections. There are also some reports of possible long-term benefits of breastfeeding for children, including a decreased risk of developing obesity, type 2 diabetes, high blood pressure and heart disease later in life (3). The benefits of breastfeeding for mothers include a decreased risk of breast and ovarian cancers, obesity, type 2 diabetes and cardiovascular disease (2, 3).

WHAT ABOUT PLANT-BASED EATING WHEN BREASTFEEDING?

This is an area of continuing and emerging research. We know from many studies that the nutritional content of breast milk can be affected by what breastfeeding mums eat, but it's not quite that straightforward! The macronutrient content of breast milk (carbohydrates, protein and total fat) is generally not affected by the foods that are eaten, unless a breastfeeding mother is severely malnourished and not eating enough calories and protein to meet her needs.

In the 1980s there was some concern about the nutritional composition of vegetarian mothers' breast milk. However, the mothers involved in the study at the time were eating a highly restrictive macrobiotic diet which is not the same as a nutritionally balanced vegetarian or vegan diet with appropriate supplementation (4). More recent research has found that the breast milk of vegetarian women is nutritionally adequate and similar in composition to omnivorous women's breast milk (5).

VITAMINS AND MINERALS IN BREAST MILK

The vitamin content of breast milk can be affected by what the person producing it has eaten. This is particularly true for vitamins A, C, B12 and B6, as well as a type of essential fat called DHA (more about this nutrient below). On the other hand, the mineral content of breast milk is generally not affected as much by food. For example, the iron and calcium content of breast milk is not affected by the foods that have been eaten. One exception to this is the mineral iodine; the iodine content of breast milk does seem to be affected by what the person producing it has been eating (6).

DHA IN BREAST MILK

Although the TOTAL fat content of breast milk is not affected by different dietary patterns, the TYPES of fats found in breast milk can be influenced by the diet of the person breastfeeding. For example, if a breastfeeding woman regularly eats fish and seafood or regularly takes a DHA supplement, then this is reflected by a higher DHA content in her breast milk. Studies also show that although DHA supplements can increase the levels of DHA in breast milk, ALA (the precursor for DHA) does not raise breast milk DHA levels (7). Additionally, some studies have found that taking DHA supplements while breastfeeding can not only raise DHA levels in breast milk but also result in improved developmental scores of children at two and a half years of age (8).

I think the main message from these studies is that DHA supplements are particularly important for breastfeeding mums who do not eat oily fish and seafood, even if they are eating additional sources of alpha-linolenic acid (ALA) such as walnuts, tofu, flaxseed, hemp seeds, chia seeds and their oils. This is because the research shows that these sources of ALA do not sufficiently raise DHA levels within breast milk. DHA is particularly important for babies as it plays a crucial role in their brain and eye development. In my professional opinion, based on what I have read, I feel that pregnant and breastfeeding women and children under the age of two are the three groups that are particularly vulnerable to low DHA levels and would therefore benefit from DHA supplements. Algal oil supplements are vegan, and you can find out more about supplements in the table at the end of this chapter. If you'd like to read about essential fats and DHA, there is more detail in Chapter 3.

Iodine in the diet and breast milk composition

The iodine content of breast milk can be affected by what the people producing it are eating. This is especially important in plant-based breastfeeding mums as their eating pattern could be low in iodine. The main sources of iodine in a typical UK diet are cow's milk, dairy products, eggs, and fish or seafood. If you are not eating any of these foods, then I would recommend an iodine supplement (see the table at the end of this chapter for suggested amounts).

A recent study looking at the iodine concentration of breast milk in mothers eating vegan, vegetarian and omnivorous diets found that the vegan and vegetarian participants' breast milk had lower iodine concentrations than that of the omnivorous group. This was a small study involving only 30 women, so we should interpret the results with caution. However, it does provide some evidence that it is important to consider the iodine intake of breastfeeding mothers and supplement appropriately (9). Another study also found lower levels of iodine in the breast milk of plant-based mothers, with vegan mothers' breast milk having the lowest levels, followed by vegetarians and omnivores (10, 11).

Some fortified dairy alternative drinks and yoghurts contain iodine and therefore could be a source of iodine for people who are breastfeeding. Check the label of your dairy alternative drink to see if it contains added iodine. The amount added varies greatly between different brands; some contain only 13µg per 100ml, whereas others contain as much as 30µg per 100ml. As breastfeeding mothers need 200µg iodine per day, even if you drank 500ml of a plant-based drink fortified with 30µg of iodine per 100ml each day, this would only supply 150µg of iodine, so an iodine supplement is likely to be needed for most plant-based breastfeeding mothers.

In a nutshell...

Based on all the research we have so far, it is important to ensure that breastfeeding women who are eating a mostly plant-based diet have adequate iodine intakes. If you exclude dairy products, eggs and fish or seafood from your diet – or only eat them very rarely (once a month or less) – then I would recommend an iodine supplement as a reliable way of ensuring that you are getting enough iodine (but also not too much). This is especially important in the UK where salt is not routinely iodised, which means that the salt available in supermarkets is not a source of iodine.

WHAT SHOULD I EAT TO SUPPORT BREASTFEEDING?

During breastfeeding, your nutritional needs increase in order to support your body with the demands of producing breast milk for your baby. But don't worry, you don't need to eat a special diet while breastfeeding, just a healthy balanced diet with perhaps an extra snack each day as your energy and protein needs will be slightly higher, especially during the first six months of breastfeeding. This will likely be reflected by an increase in your appetite. I remember feeling incredibly hungry when I was breastfeeding my girls, even waking up at night feeling starving! So, it can be helpful to have some nutritious snacks on hand to reach for when you need an energy boost. If you receive any offers of help with food from family or friends, my recommendation would be to accept them! Having your freezer stocked with healthy meals that you can simply pop in the oven is so helpful when you are breastfeeding and short of time (and sleep!).

WHAT DOES A HEALTHY BALANCED DIET LOOK LIKE?

Eat the rainbow! Include plenty of fruits and vegetables in your diet: try to include as much variety as you can, choosing fruits and vegetables of all the colours of the rainbow. This will ensure that you are receiving a variety of nutrients, as different colours mean different vitamins and minerals.

Don't skimp on carbs! Your body needs energy to support the demands of breastfeeding, so include starchy carbohydrates at each meal and snack. Examples include oats, wholemeal bread, brown rice, quinoa, pasta and potatoes.

Power up! Your body needs good sources of protein, such as tofu, nuts, seeds, nut butters, lentils, beans, and soya milk. Dairy products, eggs, fish, and seafood are also good sources of protein if you include those foods in your eating pattern. If you eat oily fish, you should limit this to a maximum of two portions (around 140g each) per week, as these can contain pollutants that can reach your breast milk.

During breastfeeding, there are certain nutrients that women need additional quantities of. Most of the increased quantities of vitamins and minerals can be achieved by eating slightly more food, which is easily done by incorporating one or two healthy snacks into your daily eating pattern. However, I think there are a few nutrients that require special consideration for plant-based breastfeeding women, as follows:

Calcium: requirements are high at 1250mg per day (an additional 550mg)

Vitamin A: requirements are high at 950µg per day (an additional 350µg)

Zinc: requirements are high at 13mg per day (an additional 6mg)

Vitamin B12: supplement recommended (as there are no plant-based sources, unless fortified)

Iodine: supplement recommended (as there are very few plant-based sources)

The table below gives you a breakdown of the additional amounts of nutrients that are recommended during breastfeeding. These are national recommendations for ALL breastfeeding women, not only those who are plant-based. Please note that the amounts below are in addition to the amounts recommended for adult women who are not pregnant or breastfeeding, which are shown in the second column.

NUTRIENT	ADULT WOMEN 19–50 YEARS (NOT PREGNANT OR BREASTFEEDING)	BREASTFEEDING 0–4 MONTHS	BREASTFEEDING 4+ MONTHS
Energy/calories	Varies depending on activity levels	+330-500 calories	+330 calories
Protein*	Varies depending on body weight	+11g	+8g
Vitamin A	600µg	+350µg	+350µg
Vitamin B1	0.8mg	+0.2mg	+0.2mg
Vitamin B2	1.1mg	+0.5mg	+0.5mg
Vitamin B3	13mg	+2mg	+2mg
Vitamin B12**	1.5µg	+0.5µg	+0.5µg
Folate	200µg	+60µg	+60µg
Vitamin C	40mg	+30mg	+30mg
Calcium	700mg	+550mg	+550mg
Zinc	7mg	+6mg	+2.5mg
Copper	1.2mg	+0.3mg	+0.3mg
Selenium	60µg	+15µg	+15µg
Iodine	140µg	***	***

*For protein, the recommended amounts are an extra 11g per day from 0 to 6 months and an extra 8g per day for 6+ months.

**Plant-based breastfeeding mums require vitamin B12 supplements of 10-25µg (see table on supplements at the end of this chapter).

***No additional iodine is recommended in the UK during breastfeeding. However, Plant Based Health Professionals UK recommends 150-200µg iodine per day for plant-based breastfeeding mums.

NUTRITIOUS SNACK IDEAS

Here are some ideas for delicious and nutritious snacks that all provide around 300 calories and 8-11g of protein, which provides the additional energy and protein recommended when breastfeeding. Always listen to your appetite though; the quantities stated below are just suggestions.

Smoothies (see my recipes on page 220)

A portion of hummus with pitta bread and fruit

1 wholemeal bagel with peanut butter and banana

2 slices of wholemeal toast with almond butter and strawberries

2 Super Seeded Breakfast Cookies (see recipe on page 174) with 300ml of soya milk

1 Lemon and Blueberry Flapjack (see recipe on page 216)

½ an avocado, sliced or smashed, on 2 slices of wholemeal toast

A salad containing ½ an avocado, 1 tomato, 50g of tofu or mozzarella (if you eat dairy products) and 1 tbsp of olive oil dressing

How to ensure you're meeting your increased nutrient requirements

VITAMIN A: Choose fruits and vegetables rich in beta-carotene each day, such as red, orange or yellow peppers, mangoes, papayas, apricots, carrots, and sweet potatoes, as well as leafy green vegetables. These foods will help you meet the increased vitamin A requirements while breastfeeding. Remember that beta-carotene is converted to vitamin A in your body.

PROTEIN: Make sure you have a source of protein at each of your meals. Soya- or pea-based dairy alternatives, tofu or tempeh, edamame beans, lentils, beans, nuts and seeds are all examples of good plant-based sources of protein. Meat alternatives can also be a good option and provide some variety in your diet, though be aware that these products may contain added salt, so try not to eat them more than once per day. Examples include Quorn® mince (made from mycoprotein), soya burgers or sausages, and products made with pea protein such as sausages, burgers and meatballs.

CALCIUM: Choose calcium-fortified dairy alternative drinks and yoghurts, calcium-set tofu and green leafy vegetables such as broccoli, kale, pak choi, watercress, and spring greens to help you meet your calcium requirements. Many breastfeeding supplements also contain calcium as part of their nutritional profile (please check the label). Breastfeeding mothers need an additional 550mg of calcium per day, on top of the 700mg calcium recommended for adult females, for a total of 1250mg calcium per day.

ZINC: Good sources of zinc include nutritional yeast, nuts and seeds, quinoa, wholemeal bread, tofu, chickpeas, lentils, and red kidney beans. Just 5g of nutritional yeast contains 6mg of zinc!

Are there any foods I need to avoid while breastfeeding?

Not unless you are allergic to a particular food yourself. In fact, research has shown that the flavour of foods you eat during pregnancy and breastfeeding can be transferred to your baby, so they may enjoy those foods more when they are introduced to solids (12). However, oily fish should be limited to two servings per week (around 140g is a serving). Peanuts and other food allergens (dairy products, eggs, tree nuts, soya, wheat, sesame, fish and shellfish) can be included in your eating pattern and there is no evidence that this increases the chance of your baby being allergic to these foods. On the contrary, research shows that if a breastfeeding mother eats peanuts while breastfeeding and introduces peanuts (as smooth peanut butter or ground peanuts) to her baby within their first year of life, this may reduce the risk of that child developing a peanut allergy (13). It's also worth noting here that many women may choose to stop drinking alcohol completely while breastfeeding. However, occasional small amounts of alcoholic drinks can be included without any adverse effects on your baby (14).

Dietary recommendations for breastfeeding mothers

Remember to include in your diet:

CAROTENOID-RICH

Sweet Potato
Carrot
Pumpkin
Spinach
Peppers

CALCIUM-RICH

Green Vegetables
Kale
Broccoli
Calcium-set Tofu
Fortified Plant Milks
Legumes
Chia Seeds
Sesame Seeds
Almonds

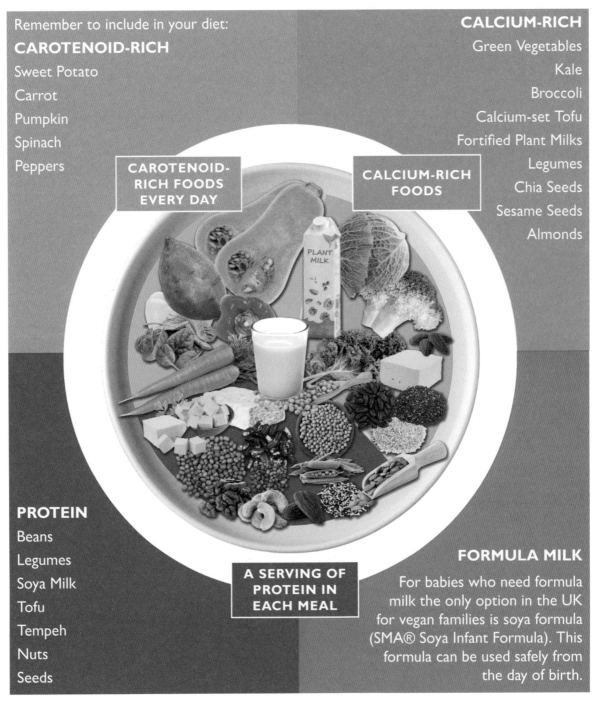

CAROTENOID-RICH FOODS EVERY DAY

CALCIUM-RICH FOODS

A SERVING OF PROTEIN IN EACH MEAL

PROTEIN

Beans
Legumes
Soya Milk
Tofu
Tempeh
Nuts
Seeds

FORMULA MILK

For babies who need formula milk the only option in the UK for vegan families is soya formula (SMA® Soya Infant Formula). This formula can be used safely from the day of birth.

Source: 24

CAN MY BABY BE ALLERGIC TO MY BREAST MILK?

Not as such, but your baby could be allergic to food proteins that are passed into breast milk. For example, if your baby is allergic to a particular food protein, such as cow's milk protein, you may be advised by your healthcare team to avoid cow's milk and dairy products while breastfeeding, as food proteins can be transferred to breast milk. Around 0.5-1% of breastfeeding babies are allergic to cow's milk protein (compared to around 2-7.5% of formula-fed babies) (15). However, many babies who are allergic to cow's milk protein (or other food proteins) may still be able to tolerate the tiny amounts of proteins that are passed through breast milk, so please discuss with your healthcare professional before eliminating any particular foods from your diet.

SUPPLEMENTS FOR YOU AND YOUR BABY

These recommendations are for all babies and young children, regardless of their eating pattern. The NHS recommends that all breastfed babies are given a vitamin D supplement of 8.5-10µg per day from birth, and 10µg per day from six months onwards. This is recommended in addition to any supplement that the person breastfeeding them is taking, so remember to start your baby on vitamin D drops as soon as you can. From six months to five years of age, the NHS also recommends a vitamin A supplement of 233µg per day for breastfed or combination fed babies (16).

Note that babies who are drinking more than 500ml of infant formula per day do not need supplements, as the infant formula already contains additional amounts of vitamins A and D. If a baby is being fed a combination of breast milk and formula milk, then they should be given supplements if the intake of formula is less than 500ml per 24-hour period.

The table overleaf is a summary of the recommended supplements for plant-based babies, toddlers and breastfeeding women (17, 18). Please note that these are IN ADDITION to the supplements of vitamins A and D that are recommended in the UK for all babies and young children from six months to five years of age, regardless of eating pattern.

NUTRIENT	RECOMMENDED DAILY AMOUNT
VITAMIN B12	
Breastfeeding	10-25µg
0-6 months	Breast milk or infant formula*
7-12 months	2.5-5µg when eating 3 meals per day
1-3 years	2.5-5µg
4-6 years	5µg
IODINE	
Breastfeeding	150-200µg**
0-6 months	Breast milk or infant formula*
7-12 months	Breast milk or infant formula*
1-3 years	50-70µg
4-6 years	100µg
DHA/EPA (omega-3 fats)	
Breastfeeding	400-500mg (with at least 250mg being DHA)
0-6 months	Breast milk or infant formula*
7-12 months	Breast milk or infant formula*
1-2 years	10-12mg/kg DHA
2-4 years	100-150mg DHA+EPA
4-6 years	150-200mg DHA+EPA

*As long as the baby is breastfeeding on demand and the mother is taking a supplement with vitamin B12, iodine and DHA/EPA or eating foods with adequate levels of these nutrients.

**Recommended by Plant Based Health Professionals UK. The WHO recommends 250µg of iodine per day for breastfeeding mothers.

FORMULA FEEDING

If you are unable to breastfeed or you would like to combination feed, you will need an appropriate infant formula for your baby. Breast milk or infant formula are the only suitable main drinks for all babies under the age of 12 months. Most infant formulas available in the UK are made from modified cow's milk or goat's milk; there are no fully vegan infant formulas currently available in the UK. The closest infant formula to being fully plant-based is SMA soya infant formula, which is classified as vegetarian but not vegan because the source of vitamin D in the formula is from lanolin in sheep's wool. This is the only brand of soya formula currently available in the UK (19).

The NHS currently does not recommend soya infant formula for babies under the age of six months as a precautionary measure (20, 21). Other countries tend to use soya infant formula more frequently than the UK. For example, it has been reported that 25% of babies in the US and 20% in Canada are fed using a soya formula (22). However, the British Dietetic Association Paediatric Group statement on soya recognises that for vegan mothers who are not able to breastfeed, soya infant formula is the only nutritionally adequate formula available that aligns with their lifestyle choice (23). Plant Based Health Professionals UK state that soya infant formula can safely be used from the day of birth (24).

SO, IS SOYA FORMULA SAFE FOR MY BABY?

This is an area of continuing debate and there is no universal agreement between health professionals around the world. There has been some controversy about soya in the past, mainly due to animal studies. However, more recent research on humans has shown that we metabolise (absorb and break down) isoflavones or phytoestrogens within soya very differently to animals (25). There has also been a major review of soya infant formula, combining many studies into what is called a systematic review with meta-analysis. This is a way of gaining a better and deeper understanding of a particular topic as there are more participants involved. In the analysis, they found that babies born at full term and a good birth weight who were fed soya infant formula grew normally, had good bone strength (bone mineralisation) and normal immune development. In addition, the review found no evidence of any significant effects on the reproductive function in humans (26).

There are a few circumstances when soya infant formula is not appropriate, including for premature babies, those with kidney failure, and those on thyroid medication. Conversely, there are also certain medical conditions and circumstances in which soya infant formula is the most suitable option for feeding babies, including galactosaemia, hereditary lactase deficiency, and when a vegan diet is preferred (22, 27).

IMPORTANT: NEVER BE TEMPTED TO MAKE YOUR OWN FORMULA!

One thing that must be avoided completely is homemade formulas. There have been reports in the past of parents making formulas themselves, but these are highly unsafe, and babies have been hospitalised from being fed these homemade formulas. The composition of infant formulas is highly regulated and must comply with very stringent safety and nutritional criteria to be safe for babies to consume. There have been many homemade formula recipes available online or on social media in the past few years but please be aware that these are NOT safe or recommended and they can have serious consequences for your baby's health. Please do not be tempted to make your own formula! If you are unsure about anything or worried that your baby may not be tolerating their formula, speak with a health professional (28, 29).

WHAT IF MY BABY IS ALLERGIC TO COW'S MILK PROTEIN AND/OR SOYA PROTEIN?

If your baby is allergic to cow's milk protein and/or soya protein, and you are not breastfeeding exclusively, it is important that they are given an appropriate infant formula such as an extensively hydrolysed or amino acid formula. The first line treatment for babies under six months of age with cow's milk protein allergy (who are not breastfed) is an extensively hydrolysed formula (30). Please speak with your GP if you would like further information or for a referral to a paediatric dietitian and/or specialist allergy team.

CASE STUDY

Cassie approached me as she wanted some help with planning her nutrition while breastfeeding her three-month-old daughter. Cassie had been vegan for many years and felt that she knew what to eat for her own health but, as she was breastfeeding, she wanted to make sure that she was optimising her nutrition for her daughter.

We discussed Cassie's eating pattern; she would generally eat three meals and two or three snacks per day. Cassie would start the day with a large smoothie made with banana, strawberries, flaxseed, dates and water. At mid-morning she would have a handful of nuts and for lunch a large salad with avocado, cucumber, tomatoes and bulgur wheat with an olive oil dressing. For a mid-afternoon snack she would eat a large bowl of fruit and then dinner would be stir-fried tofu, vegetables and noodles with a peanut sauce. Later in the evening she would snack on nuts and dark chocolate. Cassie also took a vegan multivitamin, which didn't contain any calcium or iodine.

MY ASSESSMENT

Cassie had a very healthy diet full of fruits, vegetables, nuts, seeds, and wholegrains but her diet was low in calcium and could also be slightly low in protein. Breastfeeding mums have very high calcium requirements of 1250mg per day as well as increased protein requirements (an additional 11g per day in the first four months).

MY RECOMMENDATIONS

- **Swap to a multivitamin and mineral supplement that contains calcium and iodine as well as at least 10-25µg of vitamin B12.**

- **Add a fortified soya- or pea-based drink to the morning smoothie and add a portion of fortified soya yoghurt to the mid-morning snack of nuts, increasing both the calcium and protein intake.**

- **Have a bowl of porridge made with a scoop of Ready Oats in the morning to further increase the calcium and protein intake.**

- **Start a DHA/EPA supplement of 400-500mg per day, to include at least 250mg of DHA.**

- **Make sure that the tofu is calcium-set as an additional source of calcium.**

I think this case illustrates the fact that breastfeeding women have unique nutritional requirements, particularly for calcium, as an additional 550mg of calcium is recommended (on top of the 700mg of calcium recommended for adult women). It is also very important to ensure that vegan breastfeeding women take sufficient supplemental vitamin B12 as this nutrient is not found within plant foods (unless they are fortified). Speaking with a registered dietitian with additional training in plant-based nutrition can be helpful when you are breastfeeding, to make sure your unique nutritional requirements are being met so that you can provide optimal nourishment for your baby.

CHAPTER 5
Plant Powered Tots

Chapter 5
Plant Powered Tots

FEEDING YOUR PLANT-POWERED BABY FROM 6-12 MONTHS OF AGE

Introducing solids to your baby is a very exciting time in their development. However, it can also feel like an overwhelming and extremely daunting task. You probably feel like you have just got the hang of breastfeeding or bottle feeding your baby and now there is something else to think about! If you are wanting to raise your baby plant-based or mostly plant-based, you may be feeling even more anxious about this next step. You may even have family members and friends who have advised you not to feed your baby this way. After reading this chapter, I hope that you will feel more confident and relaxed about introducing solids to your plant-based baby with the knowledge and insights that you have gained. There is no "perfect" way to feed a baby and I think it is important that every parent or carer feels comfortable that the way they choose to feed their baby aligns with their cultural and personal views. Let's get stuck in!

INTRODUCING SOLIDS TO YOUR BABY (OR COMPLEMENTARY FEEDING)

In the UK, we tend to refer to introducing solids to babies as 'weaning'. However, there has been a move away from this word as this implies weaning off or stopping something, which is not what should be happening during this time. When introducing solids to babies, breast milk or formula milk is still a very important part of their nutrition, and the transition from milk feeds to solid food should be slow and gradual over a long period of time (at least six months). Breastfeeding is recommended up to two years of age and beyond by the World Health Organisation (WHO).

The WHO refers to introducing solids as 'complementary feeding' because the food and nutrients provided should complement the nutrition received from milk feeds (1). They define complementary feeding as: "The process starting when breast milk alone is no longer sufficient to meet the nutritional needs of infants and therefore other foods and liquids are needed, ALONGSIDE breast milk." The British Dietetic Association (BDA) defines complementary feeding as: "The introduction of solid foods into the diet of a baby who is drinking breast milk or formula milk. It is a GRADUAL process, but by the time they are one year old, most children will be eating chopped, mashed family food."

You can see that I have emphasised the words "alongside" and "gradual" as it is SO important that your baby still receives their milk feeds (whether breast or formula milk) with solid foods offered alongside this. Complementary feeding is a very gradual process, whereby small tastes of food are offered initially once per day and gradually increased as your baby learns the skills of feeding (biting, chewing, moving foods around in their mouth, and swallowing) and the volume of food that they can manage increases. This is a very gradual process and each baby is different, so I recommend following your baby's lead in terms of the pace of introducing solid foods.

WHY DO BABIES NEED SOLID FOODS?

Of course, we all know that babies cannot live their entire lives on milk feeds alone, but what are the actual reasons behind their need for solid foods? There are both developmental and nutritional reasons why babies need solid foods to be introduced to them. Developmental reasons include learning how to bite and chew foods, using different muscles around the mouth, developing jaw strength, using the tongue to move food around the mouth, and developing motor skills when reaching for foods and bringing them to the mouth. Encouraging babies to self-feed has been positively linked to child language development (2).

One of the main nutritional reasons for introducing solids is the need for iron. Iron is a critical nutrient for babies and young children as it has so many important functions in the body (see Chapter 3 for more details). Babies are born with enough iron stores to last around six months (if full term and a good birth weight) and after this age, iron stores start to deplete (3). Breast milk contains very little iron, so from the age of six months, additional iron in the form of iron-rich foods needs to be introduced to babies so that they don't become iron deficient. Another nutritional reason for introducing solids is the fact that beyond six months of age, breast milk or formula milk can no longer provide all the energy that babies need as they grow very rapidly during their first year of life.

How do I know when my baby is ready to start trying solid foods?

If you are feeling confused about when to start introducing solids to your baby, you are not alone! A survey of 1,000 parents of babies aged three to 18 months of age conducted by the Office for Health Improvement and Disparities (OHID) in the UK in 2022 found that 40% of parents felt unsure as to what age to start introducing solid foods to their baby. The OHID survey also found that almost two thirds (64%) of parents had received conflicting advice about when to start introducing solid foods to their baby (4). So, it's no wonder you're confused!

When I am presenting weaning workshops, this is a question that always comes up and a very good one. You may be thinking of a specific age that your baby is going to be ready for solids, but I recommend looking at your baby instead of the calendar, as all babies develop at different rates. What I mean by that is looking for signs that your baby is developmentally ready for solids (5). Signs of this developmental readiness include your baby being able to:

- **Sit up with minimal support**
- **Hold their head and neck in a stable position**
- **Reach out, pick up and bring objects to the mouth**
- **Swallow food, rather than push it back out (also known as the tongue thrust reflex)**

Some common developmental signs that are often mistaken for signs of readiness include:

- **Starting to wake more frequently at night**
- **Seeming hungrier than usual**
- **Starting to suck fists and chew things**
- **Showing an interest in food when parents are eating**

These are all very normal and healthy behaviours for babies, but they are not necessarily signs that your baby is ready for solids.

Starting solids and allergy prevention

If your baby is at increased risk of developing a food allergy – defined as babies who have early onset eczema or those who already have a food allergy (such as cow's milk protein allergy) – the evidence for introducing solids earlier (between four and six months of age) is compelling. If this applies to your baby, I recommend speaking with a health professional, preferably an allergy specialist, to come up with an individual plan for introducing them to solids, particularly peanuts and eggs, between the ages of four and six months. Babies who are considered at increased risk of developing a food allergy stand to benefit the most from early introduction of these allergens, which has the potential to prevent the development of allergies to those foods later in life (6).

The question of whether babies who are not considered at high risk of developing food allergies (the 'general population') should be introduced to peanuts and eggs between four and six months is still being debated. A paper was published in 2023 suggesting that we should be introducing peanuts (as ground nuts or thinned out smooth peanut butter) to babies somewhere between four and six months of age to have the biggest impact on reducing peanut allergies at a population level (7). However, this is not currently the NHS policy, and at the time of writing, the advice remains to introduce solids when your baby is developmentally ready, which is usually around six months for most babies, and to introduce peanuts and well-cooked eggs after their first tastes of solid foods (8).

WHEN IS IT TOO EARLY TO START SOLIDS?

As mentioned above, it is best to look at your baby and assess whether they are showing the signs of developmental readiness for starting to introduce solids, rather than relying on a particular age, as all babies develop at different rates. Starting solids too early can increase the risk of your baby developing an infectious illness such as gastroenteritis (tummy bug) as well as ear or chest infections (9). Starting solids before the age of four months or 17 weeks is not recommended (10).

WHEN IS IT TOO LATE TO START SOLIDS?

Delaying the introduction of solids beyond seven months of age is not recommended as this can increase the risk of your baby becoming iron deficient, especially if they are breastfed (10). This is why I recommend the introduction of iron-rich foods early on when starting solids. There is some research to suggest that the longer you wait to introduce lumpy or more textured foods (beyond nine to ten months of age), the harder it can be to introduce these foods to your baby. So, don't delay this stage of introducing solid foods; you can start by gradually thickening up purées, blending foods more briefly so that small lumps are left, mashing foods with a fork instead of blending, and introducing foods with a grainy texture such as couscous (11).

IN A NUTSHELL...

Considering all the evidence and recommendations, I think it is important to look for the signs that your baby is developmentally ready when thinking about when to introduce solid foods.

Prioritise iron-rich foods when starting to introduce solids to your baby.

Introduce allergenic foods, particularly peanuts and eggs (if your family includes them), early in your little one's weaning journey – within the first few weeks if possible.

Starting solids before 17 weeks of age is not recommended and nor is waiting beyond seven months of age, so somewhere within this window is ideal.

What method is best for introducing solids? Should I do baby-led weaning or spoon feeding?

Start by offering solid food to your baby once a day. Choose a time of day when your baby is not too hungry or too tired. Around half an hour after a milk feed is ideal, but not when they are due a nap. There is no single best method of feeding your baby, and the research does not support one particular way of introducing solids. It is important that you feel comfortable with the method of feeding that you choose, and remember that you don't need to pick just one approach, as you can do a combination of purées and finger foods. I think a combination approach of puréed or mashed foods and soft finger foods works well for most babies, as it gives them plenty of opportunities to try foods of different textures.

I also think it is important to have the right expectations about the early days of introducing solids. In the first few weeks and months of introducing solids to your baby, don't expect them to eat very much food! Focus on the VARIETY as opposed to the VOLUME of food that your baby is eating. Breast milk or formula milk is still providing the majority of their nutrition. My main message is to prioritise iron-rich foods for your baby.

Does baby-led weaning mean my baby won't be fussy with foods as a toddler?

No, not necessarily. There is no guarantee that your baby will not be a fussy toddler and most toddlers go through a phase of being selective with foods or food refusal, so this is in many ways typical toddler behaviour and to be expected. I think it is helpful to have this in mind so that it is not a shock if your toddler becomes selective with their foods.

However, there is research that suggests the way in which you feed your baby is more important than the method of feeding you choose. Whether or not you are using a 'responsive feeding' approach seems to have more impact than whether you are spoon-feeding or offering finger foods. Responsive feeding means watching your baby for any signs or cues they are giving to tell you that they would like more food or have had enough (12).

CUES THAT YOUR BABY WANTS MORE FOOD INCLUDE:

Opening their mouth

Leaning forward

Reaching out or pointing at finger food

Happy and smiling

Licking their lips

Flapping their arms or hands excitedly

CUES THAT YOUR BABY HAS HAD ENOUGH FOOD INCLUDE:

Turning their head away

Closing their mouth

Pushing your hand or the food away

Throwing food or the spoon

Trying to get out of the highchair

Crying or seeming distressed

LET THEM GET MESSY!

I am a huge advocate for letting your baby get messy when starting solids. This is not merely a way to create more washing for you (sorry!); there is actually a lot of science behind it (13, 14). Try to involve your baby in the feeding experience and encourage them to touch and smell foods that you offer to them. You can offer soft finger foods for your baby to pick up, pre-load a spoon and then hand it to them, or allow them to eat with their hands and scoop food up themselves. This will help your baby to learn about foods, which in turn helps them to accept a wide range of foods. It is well documented that the period between six and 12 months is a unique opportunity to introduce a wide variety of tastes and textures to babies, as they are very accepting of new flavours and textures during this time (13). It is also hugely beneficial to eat with your baby as often as you can, because babies learn by copying others and there is research to suggest that family meals are beneficial for children's long-term health and building a positive relationship with food (15).

IN A NUTSHELL...

I recommend starting to introduce solids to your baby by offering them a combination of textures as puréed foods and soft finger foods. Feeding your baby responsively – following their cues – is more important than which method of feeding you choose (spoon feeding, baby-led weaning or both).

What foods are best to start with?

There is no specific rule in terms of what food is best to start with when introducing solids. Vegetables, fruits, cereals, or protein-rich foods such as beans and lentils are all good options when starting solids. Whatever food you start with, aim to include iron-rich foods within the first few weeks of starting solids to ensure that your baby does not become iron deficient, as their own iron stores start to decrease from six months of age. I recommend offering iron-rich foods paired with foods rich in vitamin C to maximise the absorption of iron. Introducing food allergens is another important aspect of introducing solids and it is recommended to introduce the top allergens to your baby early on when starting solids, after their first tastes (see the next section of this chapter for more details).

IRON-RICH FOODS INCLUDE:

Iron-fortified cereals*

Lentils (all varieties)

Beans (all types)

Peas

Tofu or tempeh

Nut butters (smooth, thinned out with water or milk) or ground nuts

Seed butters or ground seeds

Edamame (also known as soy or soya beans)

Chickpeas and hummus

Quinoa (you can make porridge from quinoa flakes)

Oats

Green vegetables such as broccoli, kale, spinach, and spring greens (offer leafy greens as a purée from a spoon, or mixed into other foods)

*Check whether your baby's cereal is fortified with iron by looking at the ingredients list on the packaging. For example, we know Ready Brek is fortified with iron because it appears in the ingredients as follows: Wholegrain Rolled Oats (60%), Wholegrain Oat Flour (38%), Calcium, Niacin, Iron, Riboflavin (B2), Vitamin B6, Thiamin (B1), Folic Acid, Vitamin D, Vitamin B12.

Beans, lentils and peas are a difficult shape and texture to introduce, as they are too small for babies to pick up before they develop the pincer grasp at around nine months of age. So, we need to think creatively about how to introduce these foods to babies. Making lentil fritters or sweet potato burgers is a great way to do this, or you could blend beans into a dip or spread so they can be offered from a spoon or spread on a piece of toast. See my recipes for Black Bean Dip and Green Hummus on pages 230 and 232 for some ideas to start with.

Foods rich in vitamin C include broccoli, strawberries, potatoes, tomatoes, kiwi fruit, peppers, citrus fruits, and brussels sprouts. These examples are particularly high in vitamin C, but most fruits and vegetables contain it, so aim to offer a colourful food alongside the iron-rich options on the previous page.

EXAMPLES OF IRON + VITAMIN C PAIRINGS SUITABLE FOR BABIES:

Hummus + roasted pepper

Black bean dip + tomatoes (cut cherry tomatoes into quarters)

Edamame dip + broccoli

Iron-fortified porridge + kiwi fruit

Iron-fortified cereal + mango

Cashew butter on toast + strawberries

Lentil burger + potatoes

What type of finger foods are suitable for babies?

Finger foods for babies starting out with eating solids (between six and nine months of age) should be about the size of one or two adult fingers and preferably a stick shape. This is because at this age, babies use their whole fist to pick up foods (palmar grasp) and therefore those foods need to be large enough to be held while sticking out of their fist to munch on. Finger foods should also be soft enough to squish between your own thumb and forefinger, as this means the food will be soft enough for your baby's gums to break down the food in their mouth. An easy way to remember this information is the three Ss:

SIZE: 1-2 adult fingers

SHAPE: Sticks are easiest for babies to pick up with their palmar grasp

SQUISH: Soft enough to squish between your forefinger and thumb

The next stage of finger foods begins around nine months of age. From nine to ten months of age, your baby will develop the ability to pick up smaller pieces of food by bringing their thumb and forefinger together, called the pincer grasp. You can start offering smaller pieces of food during this time so that your baby can practice their pincer grasp and master their fine motor skills (11, 16, 17, 18).

Offering soft finger foods to your baby encourages their independence, development of motor skills and feeding skills such as biting, chewing and moving foods around in the mouth. There is also less risk of choking when babies are allowed to feed themselves, contrary to popular belief (19).

In a nutshell...

When starting solids, focus on offering a variety of foods and don't worry too much about the volume of foods eaten in the first few weeks or months of introducing solids.

Prioritise iron-rich foods and pair them with foods rich in vitamin C to maximise iron absorption.

Offer soft finger foods and check they are suitable by remembering the three Ss: size, shape, squish!

FOOD ALLERGIES

WHAT ARE FOOD ALLERGIES?

A food allergy is when the immune system reacts to a usually harmless food such as cow's milk, peanuts or egg. For most people, eating these food proteins (called allergens) will not cause any problems. But when people eat a food they are allergic to, the immune system considers the food allergen a threat and mounts an inappropriate response. During this response, the body releases chemicals that can result in symptoms such as swelling, itching, a rash with hives, sneezing, feeling sick and vomiting, diarrhoea, wheezing, and breathing problems. Food allergy symptoms are usually mild, especially in babies, but they can be severe and even life threatening in some cases (20).

Almost any food can cause a food allergy in theory, but there are nine foods that are responsible for around 90% of food allergies in children, known as the top nine food allergens, which are listed below:

TOP NINE FOOD ALLERGENS

COW'S MILK & DAIRY PRODUCTS

EGGS

PEANUTS

TREE NUTS

WHEAT

SOYA

SESAME

FISH

SHELLFISH

What causes food allergies?

The actual cause of food allergies is not fully understood but we do know that children with early-onset eczema (before four to six months of age) – particularly if the eczema is moderate to severe, requiring prescription medication to manage it – have an increased risk of developing a food allergy (21). The worse a baby's eczema is and the earlier it started, the more likely a food allergy is to develop. In fact, a study in Australia found that babies with eczema were six times more likely to develop an egg allergy and 11 times more likely to develop a peanut allergy when compared to babies without eczema (21).

However, it is important to point out that it is not the eczema that is causing the food allergy. Eczema is a condition where there is a problem with the skin barrier, and food proteins can sometimes be a trigger for worsening a child's eczema. It is thought that food proteins can come into contact with the immune system through the skin, which can cause a baby's immune system to become sensitised to the food proteins and then 'overreact' when these food proteins are eaten: an allergic reaction (22).

Why all the fuss about introducing allergens?

There is a growing body of evidence to suggest that introducing food allergens, particularly peanuts and (well-cooked) egg, to babies early on when introducing solids may help prevent a food allergy from developing later in life. Until 2009 in the UK, it was recommended to delay the introduction of some common allergenic foods to babies beyond one year of age and to delay the introduction of peanuts until three years of age if your family had a history of allergies. This recommendation was based on the theory that it was better to wait until a baby was older and their immune system was 'mature enough to cope' with these food allergens.

This advice has completely changed based on the research findings from many studies, particularly from the LEAP and EAT studies that took place in the UK and were published in 2015. We now understand much more about the development of food allergies and that feeding babies allergenic foods early and often within their first year of life is beneficial in terms of preventing food allergies later in life. It is now advised to introduce food allergens to babies when introducing solids and before one year of age (23, 24). There is also some research from 2022 suggesting that we should be introducing peanut products to all children before six months of age (7), not only to those at high risk of developing a peanut allergy (defined as those with early onset eczema and/or an egg allergy). However, this is not currently NHS advice and introducing the top nine allergens to all babies is recommended from around six months of age.

WHAT IS MY BABY'S LEVEL OF RISK FOR DEVELOPING A FOOD ALLERGY?

HIGHEST RISK

SEVERE ECZEMA

EXISTING FOOD ALLERGY

MILD TO MODERATE ECZEMA

BABIES WITH A FAMILY HISTORY OF ATOPY E.G ALLERGIES, ASTHMA, HAY-FEVER IN MUM/DAD/SIBLINGS

ALL OTHER BABIES "GENERAL POPULATION"

STANDARD RISK

These babies may benefit most from the early introduction of (well-cooked) egg and peanuts, between 4-6 months of age. Discuss with a health professional for support.

Slightly increased risk but not considered 'high risk'

Introduce (well-cooked) eggs and peanuts from 6 months of age, after baby's first tastes of solids, alongside a wide variety of foods. No need to delay the introduction of all common allergens.

Source: 25

You can see from the diagram above that no babies are considered at zero risk of food allergies, as all babies have a certain level of risk that we don't really know or can't quantify exactly. That is why the green section is labelled 'standard risk' as opposed to low risk or no risk of food allergies.

How do I introduce allergens?

There is no definitive consensus among health professionals on exactly how to introduce food allergens to your baby, but there are a few options that I recommend, based on the many families that I have supported over the years with introducing allergens to their baby. Let's start with some general tips:

1. Start with a SMALL amount. The smaller the quantity of food served, the less severe an allergic reaction is likely to be. Start with a small amount, such as the tip of a teaspoon of peanut butter, and increase it gradually over three or four days.

2. Introduce the new food EARLY in the day so that you can observe your baby for any possible signs of an allergic reaction. Immediate type allergic reactions usually occur within an hour (and up to 2 hours) of eating the food. If your baby has a delayed type allergy, you may choose to wait a few days before increasing the dose of the allergen.

3. Introduce each new food allergen ONE at a time, so that you can spot an allergic reaction if it occurs, and you will know which food is responsible.

4. Do not introduce a new allergen when your baby is UNWELL, such as during teething or an infection.

5. If your baby has eczema, ensure that their skin is well managed BEFORE introducing any allergens.

6. Once the allergen has been successfully introduced, continue to offer it in your baby's diet REGULARLY (at least once or twice per week).

If your baby falls within the yellow or green sections of the triangle diagram overleaf then you are encouraged to introduce the top food allergens when your baby starts solids at around six months of age, after their first tastes of food. This includes babies who may have a sibling or parent with a food allergy or other type of allergy (such as hay fever, eczema or asthma) as well as babies who have mild eczema. I usually recommend starting the introduction of allergens with peanuts (smooth peanut butter, ground peanuts or peanut puffs) or well-cooked egg, if you are going to introduce egg.

Below I have given a suggested peanut introduction plan over four days. Remember to thin down the smooth peanut butter by adding one or two teaspoons of warm water or your baby's usual milk to every teaspoon of peanut butter. Some families may want to introduce peanut quicker than this and that is fine too. This is just a suggested plan if you want to be cautious or if you are feeling a bit anxious about introducing peanuts.

DAY 1: Tip of a teaspoon of smooth peanut butter, thinned with usual milk or water as above.

DAY 2: ¼ teaspoon of smooth peanut butter, added to a previously eaten food such as porridge or a puréed fruit/vegetable.

DAY 3: ½ teaspoon smooth peanut butter, added to a previously eaten food such as porridge or a puréed fruit/vegetable.

DAY 4: 1 teaspoon smooth peanut butter, added to a previously eaten food such as porridge or a puréed fruit/vegetable.

If tolerated, aim to continue offering your baby at least 1 teaspoon of smooth peanut butter twice a week to maintain their tolerance.

What if my baby already has a diagnosed food allergy?

If your baby already has a diagnosed immediate type food allergy, such as cow's milk protein allergy, it is important to work with your Allergy Team – for example, a paediatric allergist and paediatric allergy dietitian – to come up with an individual plan for introducing allergens safely to your baby. It is not recommended that you restrict other allergenic foods from your baby's diet unless they are already allergic to these foods. Your allergist will be able to advise you if your baby needs allergy tests (skin prick tests or specific IgE blood tests) before you start introducing solids. Ideally, speak to your Allergy Team as early as possible (around three months of age) to obtain a plan for introducing solids to your baby.

What to do if you think your child is having an allergic reaction

Some babies may develop a food allergy despite your best efforts in following all the prevention advice. Although reactions are usually mild, it is important to be aware of and recognise the symptoms of an allergic reaction. If you are concerned that your baby is reacting to a certain food, stop giving them that food and seek medical advice immediately from a health professional. See the infographic overleaf for further information and advice (6).

It is also important to note that not all reactions to foods are due to an allergy. For example, some foods such as strawberries, tomatoes, citrus fruits, and aubergine can irritate the skin and cause a red rash around the mouth after eating. This is more common in babies with sensitive skin and eczema. This reaction is not a food allergy and avoiding the food is not needed. Applying a barrier cream around your baby's mouth before feeding can help prevent this type of contact reaction which may be mistaken for signs of a food allergy (20).

IMMEDIATE TYPE FOOD ALLERGY

Symptoms typically happen within 30 minutes of eating the food

MILD-MODERATE SYMPTOMS

- Swollen lips, face or eyes (angioedema)
- Itchy skin rash e.g. "Hives" (urticaria)
  - Abdominal pain
  - Vomiting

RARELY* SEVERE SYMPTOMS (ANAPHYLAXIS)

Airway: Swollen tongue, persistent cough, hoarse cry

Breathing: Difficult or noisy breathing, wheezing

Consciousness: Pale or floppy, unresponsive

risk estimated to be 1-2 per 1000 in higher risk babies

IF ANY SEVERE SYMPTOMS (ANAPHYLAXIS), IMMEDIATELY DIAL 999 FOR ASSISTANCE

- Stop the trigger food and do NOT reintroduce
- GP review recommended
- Referral to specialist care recommended for all infants presenting with symptoms of immediate-type food allergy (with access to a dietitian)

DELAYED TYPE FOOD ALLERGY

Symptoms occur >2 hours to 2-3 days after eating the food

GUT SYMPTOMS

- Recurrent abdominal pain
- Worsening vomiting/reflux
- Food refusal or aversion
- Loose/frequent stools (>6-8 times per day)

or

- Constipation/infrequent stools (2 or fewer per week)

SKIN SYMPTOMS

- Skin reddening or itch over the body
  - Worsening eczema

N.B. Delayed-type allergy cannot trigger anaphylaxis

- Stop the trigger food - symptoms should resolve after a few days
- If symptoms are not severe, consider trying the food again in 1-2 weeks
- Seek GP review if symptoms recur or are severe
- Seek advice from a dietitian
- Refer any child with persistent delayed-type symptoms (not responding to food elimination) and/or growth faltering to a specialist clinic

Source: 28

AS A PLANT-BASED FAMILY, DO WE NEED TO INTRODUCE ANIMAL ALLERGENS TO OUR BABY?

This is a question I am often asked, and one that unfortunately does not have a straightforward answer! Four out of the top nine food allergens are animal-based (dairy, egg, fish and shellfish), so this can create a dilemma for families who have chosen to raise their children as plant-based but have also read that it is important to introduce the top food allergens to babies.

As discussed above, we know that it may be beneficial to introduce allergenic foods to babies in their first year of life, as a way of helping to prevent food allergies from developing later. However, the strongest evidence we have for this preventative effect relates to peanuts (and to a lesser extent, eggs) which means that introducing peanuts and egg early on when you start introducing solids to your baby may decrease the likelihood of your little one developing peanut and egg allergies later in life (23, 24). We just don't have the evidence for ALL the food allergens yet, although it is thought that it likely will be helpful to introduce all the top allergens within the first year of life.

Of course, it's a personal decision whether you introduce these animal-based allergens to your baby or not, but here are a few of my thoughts:

Consider your baby's level of risk of developing food allergies. If your baby is at higher risk of developing food allergies (the red part of the triangle diagram on page 112) – for example, they have severe early onset eczema and/or an existing food allergy – you may wish to discuss this further with a health professional and agree a plan together. Remember that no baby is without any risk of developing food allergies.

Consider how you might continue to offer the allergen on a regular basis. Once an allergen is introduced, it needs to be offered regularly in a child's diet to maintain tolerance: at least once to twice per week. It is not enough to introduce a food a few times and then stop offering that food. We do not know exactly how long you need to keep offering the allergen, but it is likely to be several years of offering it at least once or twice per week. In the LEAP study, they continued giving peanut three times per week for five years, but that was in a group of children considered at high risk of developing a peanut allergy, so it is difficult to apply this information to all babies (24).

Consider how likely your child is to come into contact with these foods. I think it is more likely that your child might be offered foods that contain milk and/or eggs – such as cake at a birthday party – than fish or shellfish. So, you may wish to take that into account when deciding whether to introduce these foods to your baby or not.

If you decide to introduce egg to your baby, I have included a suggested egg introduction plan below. Remember to cook the egg very well; I recommend hard-boiling and serving both the white and yolk. Hard-boiled egg is a strange texture for your baby, so you may need to mash or purée it with a small amount of their usual milk for a more palatable consistency.

DAY 1: Introduce ¼ teaspoon of hard-boiled egg to your baby, added to a previously eaten food such as a puréed vegetable or fruit.

DAY 2: Increase to ½ teaspoon hard-boiled egg.

DAY 3: Increase to 1 teaspoon hard-boiled egg.

DAY 4: Increase to between one third and one half of a hard-boiled egg.

If egg is tolerated, aim to include at least half an egg twice per week in your baby's diet (1 egg across the whole week) to make sure they are not allergic to egg. Continue offering egg to your child on an ongoing weekly basis – we don't know exactly how long this is needed to be sure that they are not going to develop an allergy to egg, but it is likely to be several years.

FREQUENTLY ASKED QUESTIONS FOR THIS AGE GROUP

Q. Are there any foods that need to be avoided within the first year?

A. Yes, the following foods should be avoided for babies under 12 months of age: salt, added sugar, honey, whole nuts, popcorn, whole cherry tomatoes or grapes (these are fine if cut into quarters from around nine months of age when your baby has developed their pincer grasp) and certain fish including marlin, swordfish and shark (10).

Q. How can my baby get enough iron without eating red meat?

A. From 7-12 months of age babies need 7.8mg of iron per day (26). That's almost as much as an adult man needs! It is true that red meat such as beef, lamb and pork contains bioavailable iron but it is certainly not the only source. Beans, lentils, tofu and iron-fortified cereals can all contribute to ensuring that your little one is receiving enough iron to support their growth and development. Iron-fortified cereals are a very convenient way to offer a concentrated source of iron to babies that helps to meet their requirements. You can also bake with iron-fortified cereals and add them to porridge or overnight oats to provide an extra boost of iron (see my recipes on pages 166 and 168). Examples of iron-fortified cereals include Ready Brek (2.4mg iron per 20g) and Weetabix (2.3mg iron per 20g) or their supermarket own brand equivalents.

Q: Does my baby need to take a vitamin supplement?

A: It depends on how they are fed (breastfed or formula fed). In the UK, the government recommends that all breastfed babies receive a vitamin D supplement of 8.5-10µg per day from birth. From six months to five years of age, vitamins A and D are recommended for all breastfed babies and formula or combination fed babies who are drinking less than 500ml of infant formula per day (27). Those drinking more than 500ml of infant formula per day do not need a supplement, as the formula already contains sufficient quantities of these vitamins. See page 93 in Chapter 4 for details on the recommended amounts of vitamins A and D for your baby.

CASE STUDY 1

Nicole approached me as her 8-month-old baby Luke was not growing well and had started to drop down the percentile lines on his growth chart. Nicole had been advised by the health visitor to start adding meat to Luke's diet, as she thought that he was not getting enough protein to support his growth. Nicole was not happy about doing this as the family did not include meat in their eating pattern, but she also wanted to make sure that Luke was growing well and do the best thing for him.

When I saw Luke, I had a look at the food diary that Nicole had sent to me. Luke was breastfeeding about four to five times during the day and was being offered three meals per day. He was receiving a variety of textures, with both mashed and soft finger foods being offered. This all seemed appropriate for his age. When we discussed the type of foods that Luke was having, they were all low-fat foods such as fruit, steamed vegetables, lentils, beans, and porridge made with water as well as starchy foods such as potatoes, rice and pasta. Nicole had not introduced nut butters as she was terrified that Luke would have an allergic reaction and was not adding any oil to his foods as she had heard that seed oils were not good for children.

MY ASSESSMENT

When I assessed Luke's food diary, I found that he was not getting enough calories from his foods. His protein intake was more than adequate but his fat intake was not enough to support his growth. Fat contains a lot of calories in a small volume (nine calories per gram) whereas protein and carbohydrates contain just four calories per gram. One heaped teaspoon of peanut butter, for example, contains seven grams of fat and 90 calories. A baby of Luke's age would need around 34g of fat per day in total (this includes fat from breast milk) and 765 calories from food and breast milk combined. As you can see, foods such as nut butters or ground nuts can provide an important source of fats and calories for plant-based babies.

MY RECOMMENDATIONS

Increase the fat in Luke's diet. Practically, this meant the following actions:

- **Supporting Nicole to introduce peanuts and some tree nuts (in the form of smooth nut butters) to Luke as these would provide good sources of fat and energy.**

- **Adding seeds or seed butters to Luke's porridge as another source of fats, such as chia, flax and hemp seeds and pumpkin or sunflower seed butter.**

- **Roasting vegetables with olive or rapeseed oil for Luke instead of steaming them.**

- **Making porridge with expressed breast milk or a fortified dairy alternative containing the most fats, such as whole or 'barista' versions.**

This case study illustrates the fact that babies and young children have very different nutritional requirements to adults. For example, babies need more fats than we do as adults and therefore low-fat diets are not appropriate for babies. Fats are an important source of calories and fat-soluble vitamins for babies and young children.

CASE STUDY 2

Daisy approached me about her nine-month-old baby girl Lucy, as she was not gaining weight as well as Daisy would like her to. She had been told by her health visitor that Lucy's growth was faltering and that she should introduce Lucy to meat and dairy in order to help her put on weight. Daisy was vegan herself and wanted to raise her child on a plant-based eating pattern, although she also wanted her baby to grow and develop to her full potential, so she felt confused, conflicted and anxious. Lucy was breastfed and started on solids just before six months of age, as she was showing all the signs of developmental readiness. Daisy had followed advice that she had read online to introduce vegetables first. However, Lucy did not really take to solid foods very well. Daisy then offered fruits to Lucy and she started to take more of these, so she continued introducing fruits and added baby rice as her health visitor had advised her to do this.

MY ASSESSMENT

When I saw Lucy, I reviewed her growth chart and could see that she had dropped one percentile and her weight was heading downwards, instead of tracking on or between two percentile lines. I also reviewed her food diary to assess her nutritional intake. Lucy was only eating fruit purées and baby rice (which was not fortified with iron) and no other foods. Daisy had not introduced any iron-rich foods as she was not sure how to introduce beans or lentils due to the choking risk. She hadn't introduced any high-fat foods either, as she was worried that this could worsen her little girl's reflux.

I want to emphasise here that there is NOTHING wrong with fruits and they are very healthy foods to give your baby. Fruits contain important vitamins and minerals that are vital to babies' health and wellbeing. However, most fruits (and vegetables) contain very little fat, and many are not good sources of iron either. Fats and iron are two key nutrients for babies and fats are an important source of calories. Babies need nutrient- and energy-dense foods as the amount they eat is small, so the nutrition within each bite of food should be maximised.

MY RECOMMENDATIONS

- **Start using iron-fortified cereals such as Ready Oats or Weetabix-type cereals.**
- **Offer iron-rich foods at each meal, paired with foods rich in vitamin C to aid iron absorption. Examples include hummus and roasted pepper, Ready Oats and strawberries, nut butter on toast with kiwi fruit, and black bean dip with steamed broccoli florets.**
- **Offer foods that are rich in fats such as avocados, vegetables roasted in olive oil, nut or seed butters, ground nuts or seeds, and tofu.**
- **Eat with your baby as often as you can to increase their interest in a variety of foods and allow them to observe you eating, as babies learn by copying others.**

I think this case study highlights the importance of individualised advice; Lucy was slow to take solids initially and her mum felt anxious about this. Daisy needed support and guidance around the importance of taking your baby's lead when offering solids but also advice on how to prioritise iron-rich foods and foods that are good sources of fats to support a baby's growth and development. Offering a variety of foods is also very important to help your baby develop a taste for a wide variety of flavours and textures.

CHAPTER 6
Plant Powered Little Explorers

Chapter 6
Plant Powered
Little Explorers

EXPANDING YOUR TODDLER'S TASTES AND TEXTURES

The toddler years (between the ages of one and four) are a time of great adventure and discovery for your little one. There is so much going on for them in their development, and they are learning so many new things such as walking, talking, social skills, and independence as well as refining their eating (oral-motor) skills. In terms of toddlers and their eating, they are expanding their tastes and textures while becoming increasingly independent. I like to think of this age as the time for encouraging them to be little explorers.

When my girls were toddlers, I found it an equally challenging and rewarding time. It is such a joy to watch your child learn new skills and discover things in the world around them for the very first time, but I found the tantrums SO TOUGH to cope with and frequently felt helpless and tearful when one of my girls was kicking off, especially if the tantrum happened in a public place such as a supermarket or playground, where I could feel the judging eyes of strangers on me. Finding support from friends who had children of a similar age was an immense relief and an enormous help for me. My hope for you all is that you find your 'toddler tribe'!

TODDLERS' GROWTH IS DIFFERENT TO BABIES' GROWTH

The first 12 months of a child's life is a time of rapid growth. On average, babies triple their birth weight, grow around 25cm in length and double their brain size within their first year! After this, their growth rate slows, and children don't gain as much weight or grow as much in height over the next few years. For example, in their second year of life, toddlers gain an average of 2-3kg and grow around 10-12cm in height, while in their third year they gain around 1-2kg and grow around 5-8cm (1). Along with this slower growth rate, there is an accompanying decrease in your toddler's appetite. This can seem alarming for parents, but it is perfectly normal, and I think if you are armed with the knowledge that this is to be expected, it makes dealing with a decreased appetite easier.

Why do toddlers tend to be more selective with their food choices?

Along with a decrease in appetite, toddlers often go through a phase of food refusal or being very suspicious of new foods and even of foods they previously enjoyed. You may be wondering why this is; your little one is not merely trying to test you! I like to think of the toddler years as a 'perfect storm' that often results in your little one being more selective about the foods they will eat. Toddlers are often referred to as fussy or picky, but it is part of a toddler's normal development to go through a time of increased selectiveness, and there are several factors that contribute to this. The typical age for a toddler to start selective eating is between 18 months and two years. It peaks at around three years, and most children have outgrown this phase by five or six years old (2).

The following factors contribute to the 'perfect storm' of toddlerhood selective eating:

1. Their growth rate slows, and their appetite subsequently decreases.

2. Their independence and autonomy increases.

3. They experience food neophobia (being suspicious or wary of foods).

It is important to rule out any possible underlying medical issue if your toddler's appetite decreases significantly. Examples of underlying medical issues that could decrease appetite include constipation, iron deficiency anaemia, illness or infection, difficulties with chewing or swallowing, teething or other discomfort such as a sore throat, and enlarged tonsils. Speak with your GP or health visitor if you are worried about any of these.

Another factor that can contribute to increased fussiness at meals is an excessive intake of cow's milk or dairy alternative drinks. These drinks can fill up toddler's tummies, meaning they are not hungry for meals, so aim to limit them to around 300-400ml per day.

Strategies to help with selective eating

1. Prioritise eating together as a family as often as you can

2. Have a set meal and snack routine (see suggested routine for toddlers below)

3. Involve your children in food preparation

4. Try family-style meals, where dishes are placed in the centre of the table for each person to serve themselves (suitable for toddlers from around 18 months of age)

5. Decrease the pressure to eat at mealtimes

6. Keep offering different foods – familiarity comes with repeated exposure

7. Give toddlers some choice, such as between two different foods for a meal

8. Change how you offer the food (sometimes a food may be refused if it is cooked in a certain way but accepted if it is raw, for example)

9. Keep mealtimes fun and light-hearted

Finally, try to use the Division of Responsibility method of feeding children. The Division of Responsibility is a term coined by the dietitian Ellyn Satter which describes a method of feeding that gives parents or carers and children their own roles and responsibilities when it comes to eating (3). The parents or carers decide when, where and what will be served at mealtimes. The children decide if and how much they will eat, of the foods that are offered. Trusting that your child can decide when they have had enough to eat is a key aspect of the Division of Responsibility ethos of feeding.

This is my suggested meal and snack routine for toddlers, which aims to offer food every 2-3 hours:

Time	What to Offer
7am	Breakfast
9.30-10am	Morning Snack
12-12.30pm	Lunch
2.30-3pm	Afternoon Snack
5.30pm	Dinner
7pm	Bedtime

WHEN COULD IT BE MORE THAN TYPICAL 'FUSSY' EATING?

Most toddlers grow out of selective eating and maintain healthy growth during this period. However, in some children this is not the case. These are a few red flags to look out for:

1. Weight loss or growth faltering (dropping two or more percentiles on their growth chart)

2. Extreme distress at mealtimes

3. Persistent food refusal

4. Still having difficulties beyond the toddler years (age six and older)

5. Social isolation and/or eating alone

6. List of accepted foods becoming more and more limited, resulting in a very narrow range of accepted foods (typically less than 20)

7. Seems to refuse food even when you know they are hungry

If you recognise some of these signs in your child, I'd encourage you to ask for help; speak with your GP or health visitor who will be able to refer you to a paediatric dietitian or a specialist feeding team if needed.

KEY NUTRIENTS FOR YOUR LITTLE EXPLORERS

IRON

Iron continues to be a very important nutrient for toddlers, as their requirements are still high relative to their body size. Children aged one to three years need 6.9mg of iron per day, dropping to 6.1mg of iron per day for children between four and six (4). But don't worry, you are not expected to count the milligrams of iron in your toddler's daily diet! If you offer an iron-rich food to your toddler with every meal and maximise the absorption of iron by including good sources of vitamins C and A alongside those foods, you will be providing your toddler with the best opportunity to obtain enough iron each day. Don't worry if they sometimes eat less; toddlers' appetites vary from day to day and week to week. Try to think about their intake over a few days or a week, rather than the nutrition in each meal or day.

Here are some plant-powered meal ideas to maximise your toddler's iron absorption, most of which you can find the recipes for towards the back of this book:

Black bean dip (page 230) on a tortilla wrap with bell pepper fingers and kiwi fruit

Hummus (page 232) with pitta bread, carrot sticks and orange segments

Dal (page 180) with tomatoes and rice

Chickpea curry with rice and broccoli

Iron-fortified cereal with chia seeds, peanut butter and strawberries

Pea and mint fritters (page 196) with kiwi fruit and tomatoes

Lentil burgers (page 190) with raspberries on the side

DOES CALCIUM AFFECT IRON ABSORPTION?

Yes, calcium does seem to affect the absorption of both haem (animal-based) and non-haem forms of iron. However, the mechanism is not fully understood. Most of the research studies looking at the effect of calcium on iron absorption have shown that calcium can decrease iron absorption in a single meal, but some results have been contradictory. When studies have looked at multiple meals containing a wide variety of foods, including other inhibitors and enhancers of iron absorption, results show that calcium only has a limited effect on iron absorption (5, 6, 7).

In addition, longer term studies (between six and 12 months in duration) looking at adult women and adolescent girls found that taking a 500mg calcium supplement with meals did not have any effect on iron levels over this time period. Overall, it seems that the total amount of calcium in the diet and the presence of iron absorption enhancers (such as vitamin C and beta-carotene) is more important than the amount of calcium at any single meal (8, 9, 10).

What this means practically is that you can still offer foods rich in iron and calcium together, such as an iron-fortified cereal with a fortified dairy alternative drink or cow's milk. I recommend that children don't have excessive amounts (over 600ml per day) of fortified dairy alternatives or cow's milk though, and generally I don't recommend offering these drinks with meals as they are very filling and will likely decrease your toddler's appetite for their meal. Around 300-350ml of a fortified dairy alternative drink or cow's milk per day is enough to meet calcium requirements and shouldn't affect iron absorption or decrease appetite overall. If your little one is having less than this amount, that's fine too as long as they are having three calcium-rich foods or drinks per day (see Chapter 7 for further guidance on meal planning).

FATS

The UK recommendations for the amount of total fat that we should be eating are for children aged five years and above, so they don't apply to toddlers. For anyone over five, no more than 35% of your total calories should be obtained from fat, and saturated fat should be no more than 11% of your total calories (4, 11). Toddlers and babies, however, need more fat as a percentage of calories than older children and adults: around 35-40% which equates to 40-50g of total fats per day. You don't need to be (and I wouldn't recommend) counting calories or the grams of fat your child is having; what this means practically is offering a source of fat with most of your toddler's meals and snacks.

Examples of foods rich in fats include:

- **Avocado**
- **Olive oil**
- **Olive paste (watch the salt content)**
- **Peanut butter and ground peanuts**
- **Tree nut butters and ground nuts (such as walnuts, cashews, pistachios, almonds)**
- **Tahini (sesame seed paste)**
- **Seed butters and ground seeds**
- **Rapeseed oil**
- **Coconut oil and coconut milk (tinned)**

A NOTE ABOUT COCONUT OIL

Most plant-based sources of fats contain mostly polyunsaturated and monounsaturated sources of fats, which are considered to be the healthier forms of fats as they are associated with lower risk of heart disease. Coconuts (and palm oil) are two exceptions in the plant world as they both contain very high levels of saturated fat, which is the type of fat that we don't want to be having too much of. You can still use tinned coconut milk, in a curry for example, and coconut oil if you'd like to, but I generally wouldn't recommend coconut oil as your everyday option for frying or baking – rapeseed or olive oil are better choices for use on a daily basis.

PROTEIN

Parents often worry about their toddler's protein intake, but this is rarely a problem even in plant-based toddlers, or if your toddler is a bit on the fussy side! Toddlers don't need very much protein, just 15g per day for one- to three-year-olds and 21g per day for four- to six-year-olds (4, 12). I have given you some examples of foods that can provide this amount of protein below. Most toddlers are actually eating much more than the recommended amount of protein; a study of one- to three-year-olds found that vegan toddlers were eating 2.4 times the recommended protein intake, vegetarians 2.3 times, and the omnivore group 2.7 times the recommended daily protein intake (13). This is not a problem, although we do want to make sure that children aren't having excessive amounts of animal protein, as this has been linked to an increased risk of obesity and being overweight later in life (14).

Here are some examples of plant-based foods that provide a toddler with their daily protein intake:

- **200ml soya milk (6-7g protein) + 1 slice of bread with peanut butter (6-8g protein) + 50g cooked lentils (3g protein)**

- **2 tbsp soya yoghurt (3g protein) + 50g hummus (3g protein) + ½ a pitta bread (3g protein) + 200ml soya milk (6-7g protein)**

- **50g tofu (6-7g protein) + 60g chickpeas (4g protein) in a curry with 100g cooked rice (3g protein) + 200ml soya milk (6-7g protein)**

- **30g edamame beans (5g protein) + 200ml pea-based milk (6-7g protein) + 50g black beans (3-4g protein)**

- **For vegetarian families, if eggs and dairy are included: 1 hard-boiled egg (6g protein) + 200ml cow's milk (6g protein) + 50g hummus (3g protein)**

CALCIUM (AND VITAMIN D)

Calcium is a very important nutrient for bone health in toddlers, along with vitamin D which helps with the absorption of calcium. Toddlers between one and three years of age need 350mg of calcium per day and four- to six-year-olds need 450mg of calcium per day (4). In the UK, the NHS recommends that all children under the age of five years should have a vitamin D supplement of 10μg per day all year round, unless they are drinking more than 500ml of infant formula a day (15).

The VeChi studies showed that the vegan group of children had the lowest calcium intakes (16, 17), so we need to ensure that toddlers with plant-based eating patterns or those avoiding dairy products have an adequate calcium intake. An easy way to ensure that toddlers (who aren't breastfeeding) are receiving enough dietary calcium is to use a fortified dairy alternative drink. You can offer this as a drink and use it within foods such as over cereal, in porridge or when making a white sauce. 300ml of a fortified dairy alternative drink would provide a toddler's daily calcium requirements (if fortified at 120mg calcium per 100ml, the same amount of calcium found in cow's milk).

CALCIUM AND GREEN VEGETABLES

Broccoli is often mentioned as a good source of calcium; while this and other low oxalate green vegetables – such as kale, pak choi and watercress – are all good sources of bioavailable calcium, I think it's important to point out that the amount of these vegetables needed to meet calcium requirements is HUGE and not realistic for toddlers. For example, toddlers would need to eat 875g (almost two pounds!) of broccoli to meet the calcium requirement of 350mg per day. Broccoli and other green vegetables are very nutritious foods for many reasons, so do offer them to your children, but be aware that these foods alone are unlikely to meet calcium requirements. Fortified dairy alternative drinks and yoghurts are concentrated and convenient sources of calcium for children.

DAIRY ALTERNATIVE DRINKS, YOGHURTS AND CHEESES

All babies under the age of 12 months should have either breast milk or an infant formula as their main drink. Dairy alternatives can be used within foods but not as a main drink until at least 12 months of age. For toddlers, breast milk is still the ideal milk for your child. The World Health Organisation recommends continuing with breastfeeding until your child is two years of age and beyond, alongside the introduction of a variety of foods, including iron-rich foods (18).

There has been a huge increase in the number of dairy alternative drinks and foods available in the UK in the past few years. I believe this is due to an increasing number of people choosing to reduce their dairy intake due to the environmental impact of dairy farming. According to a survey by Mintel of 1000 people in the UK, one in three Britons (32%) are now choosing a dairy alternative drink over cow's milk and this figure is even higher (44%) among ages 25 to 44 (19). In the US, almost two thirds (64%) of adults are reported to have tried a dairy alternative drink (20).

As of July 2023, there are four dairy alternative drinks designed with toddlers in mind and marketed for one- to three-year-olds: Alpro Soya Growing Up Drink, Alpro Oat Growing Up Drink, Koko Kids Free From M!lk, and SMA Little Steps Plantygrow Drink. The following table gives you a breakdown of their nutritional composition compared to cow's milk and breast milk (please note that the sugar in cow's milk and breast milk is lactose).

Per 100ml	Full Fat Cow's Milk	Breast Milk (21)	Alpro Oat Growing Up Drink	Alpro Soya Growing Up Drink	Koko Kids Free From M!lk	SMA Little Steps Plantygrow Drink
Energy (Kcal)	66	69	60	64	53	56
Protein (g)	3.3	1.3	1.8	2.5	1.9	1
Carbohydrates (g)	4.6	7.2	5.9	8.3	1.9	7.8
Of which sugars (g)	4.6	7.2	2.5	2.5	1.9	1
Fat (g)	3.9	4.1	3.3	2.1	4.1	2.3
Salt (g)	0.11	0.04	0.11	0.04	0.11	0.04
Calcium (mg)	120	34	120	120	170	85
Iodine (µg)	31	7*	11.3	24	13	23
Iron (mg)	0.03	0.07	1.4	2.1	0.3	1.1
Vitamin D (µg)	Traces	Traces	1.5	1.5	1.2	1.7
Vitamin B12 (µg)	0.90	Traces*	0.38	0.38	0.2	0.38
Vitamin B2 (mg)	0.23	0.03*	0.21	0.21	0.5	0.2
Vitamin A (µg)	33	58*	60	0	100	62
Vitamin C (mg)	2	4*	12	12	9	14
Vitamin E (mg)	0.08	0.34*	1.3	0	3.6	0

*In breast milk, these nutrient levels may vary depending on the breastfeeding mother's diet.

The vast majority of plant-based dairy alternative drinks available in supermarkets are designed for adults and many are very low in calories and protein, particularly nut-based (almond, hazelnut, and cashew, for example) and coconut-based drinks. I generally don't recommend these dairy alternative drinks for young children. It's also important to note that dairy alternative drinks based on rice are not recommended for any children under the age of five due to the levels of arsenic that they contain. There are SO many dairy alternative drinks to choose from, so how do you choose the best option for your toddler? In my opinion, none of the dairy alternative drinks currently available are ideal for toddlers. There are many factors to consider when choosing a drink for your toddler, including:

Your child's growth – are they struggling with weight gain?

The rest of your child's diet – do they eat a variety of foods?

Other fortified foods – do they eat other fortified dairy alternatives such as yoghurts or cheeses?

Other foods included – does your child also include dairy products in their diet?

Cost of the dairy alternative drink – does the cost of your chosen drink fit into your family's budget?

To help you, I have devised a checklist for choosing a dairy alternative drink for your toddler. Use the acronym 'EPIC-V' to look for these nutrients per 100ml:

E = energy: around 40 calories or more

P = protein: around 2g or more

I = iodine: ideally around 20-30ug

C = calcium: ideally around 120mg

V = vitamins: fortified with vitamins B12 and B2

As an additional consideration, you may want to check whether the dairy alternative drink is unsweetened or low sugar (<2g added sugar per 100ml).

I recommend three portions of calcium-rich foods per day for one- to three-year-olds, and four portions for four- to six-year-olds. One portion could be any of the following:

> 200ml breast milk (see note below)
>
> 100-120ml cow's milk or fortified dairy alternative drink
>
> 100-120g yoghurt or fortified dairy alternative yoghurt
>
> 15g cheese or fortified dairy alternative cheese (the amount of calcium in fortified cheeses varies hugely – please check the label)
>
> 25g calcium-set tofu (such as Cauldron brand tofu in the UK)

NOTE: If your toddler is breastfeeding, you will probably not know the volume of breast milk they are drinking. If your toddler is breastfeeding three or four times a day, then I would recommend offering them one or two portions of other calcium-rich foods per day, such as a fortified yoghurt or calcium-set tofu, in addition to their usual breastfeeds.

See Chapter 7 for more information on meal planning to include your toddler's daily calcium requirements.

What about additives in dairy alternative drinks?

There's a lot of scary talk in the media about food additives such as emulsifiers, stabilisers and gelling agents in dairy alternative drinks and their alleged effect on our health. Food additives need to be approved by the Food Standards Agency in the UK before they can be used within foods (21) and the term 'food additives' is very broad. It includes lots of different ingredients that are used within foods for their functional properties, such as improving texture, thickening, making sure certain ingredients don't separate, enhancing a particular flavour, or ensuring the food does not go off. Some examples of these food additives include emulsifiers, stabilisers, acidity regulators, thickeners, flavour enhancers, and preservatives, among many more.

Most of the research on food additives and gut health has been in animals, so it is difficult to apply the data from these studies to humans. A recent review article about emulsifiers specifically concluded that "There is limited evidence to directly link emulsifiers and thickeners to human disease, but multiple potential pathogenic mechanisms. Knowledge of actual dietary intake and high-quality interventional studies is needed to enable the risks associated with their intake to be understood" (22). The take-home message here is that there are potential and theoretical health risks for humans with emulsifiers and thickeners, but more research in humans is needed. From all the research that I have read and reviewed, it seems that there are potential health problems associated with some food additives but not all, and there is lots of research ongoing as we still have lots of unanswered questions around this subject.

As a general guide, I would try to limit the following emulsifiers as much as possible: polysorbate 80 or 60, carboxymethylcellulose (CMC) and carrageenan. Please don't worry if your child has had foods with these emulsifiers in them though; their overall diet is more important. If your little one is eating a wide variety of fruits, vegetables, nuts, seeds, legumes, and wholegrains, they are getting plenty of 'gut healthy' beneficial substances from their foods. Fortified dairy alternative drinks also provide vitally important nutrients for growing children, such as calcium, vitamin D and iodine.

While I am not saying that we should completely ignore the research that is emerging (23, 24, 25), I don't think we need to be overly worried about additives. Certain emulsifiers such as lecithin and thickeners such as guar gum don't appear to be harmful, but I do think it is sensible to limit (as much as possible) the emulsifiers mentioned above, which are mostly present in ultra-processed foods.

SOYA

A soya bean (or soybean) is a type of legume which originates from East Asia. Soya beans are a rich source of protein and iron and are relatively high in fats, especially when compared to other legumes which are mostly very low in fat. They contain mainly polyunsaturated and monounsaturated fats, with a small amount of saturated fat (more of the beneficial types and less of the harmful fat). In short, the nutritional profile of soya beans is excellent! Soya is available in fermented and unfermented forms. Fermented forms of soya include natto, tempeh, miso (which is very high in salt) and yoghurt alternatives. The unfermented, and perhaps more common, forms of soya include edamame beans, tofu and soya milk.

WHY IS THERE SO MUCH CONTROVERSY AROUND SOYA?

The reason that soya has been shrouded in so much controversy over the past few decades is because it is a rich source of isoflavones, which are also called phyto-oestrogens (plant oestrogens). People often hear the word oestrogen and assume that this compound is the same as human oestrogen, but that's not the case. The chemical structure of isoflavones is similar to, but not the same as, the human hormone oestrogen. The small differences between isoflavones and human oestrogen mean that they have very different effects in our body.

This is where it gets a bit science-y so bear with me! There are two oestrogen receptors in the body – alpha and beta – and isoflavones can bind to both these receptors. Alpha and beta oestrogen receptors are found in lots of different organs in the body. Isoflavones found in soya prefer to bind to the beta receptor, whereas human oestrogen has no preference (it binds equally well to alpha and beta oestrogen receptors). Because isoflavones can weakly bind to alpha oestrogen receptors, this means that they can exert very weak oestrogen effects, such as decreasing the occurrence of hot flushes in women going through the menopause. But because isoflavones prefer to bind to the beta receptors, they can also produce effects in the body that are opposite to the effects of oestrogen, such as being protective against certain types of cancers, especially if soya foods are eaten in early childhood (26, 27, 28).

Is soya safe to give to my children?

Yes, definitely! In fact, the research suggests that eating soya foods and drinking soya milk is not only safe but actually beneficial for children (26). In the UK, the advice is that you can safely introduce soya foods from six months of age as part of a healthy, balanced diet (29). A review published in 2022 looked at over 400 studies investigating the safety of soya and isoflavones in adults and children (30). This comprehensive review concluded that "there is little evidence to suggest that isoflavones, when consumed at levels not exceeding Asian intake (<100mg per day which is equivalent to 850ml of soya milk per day), exert untoward effects in adults". There are fewer studies on soya involving children but those that were conducted found that soya and isoflavone intake in children is safe and that no clinically relevant effects of soya and isoflavones on children's hormones have been found (31, 32).

How much soya should I offer my little one?

Soya foods and drinks can form part of a healthy, balanced plant-based eating pattern and they are an important source of protein, fats, and (if fortified) calcium. In the review of soya foods and isoflavones mentioned above, the authors suggest an upper limit of 50mg isoflavones per day, which equates to around 430ml of soya drink or 100g of tofu per day as a maximum. The authors stress that the upper limit does not suggest an adverse effect above this level, as no evidence of harm has been demonstrated in humans. This recommendation is half of the upper limit suggested for adults and is suggested as a reasonable intake to maintain variety in the rest of the diet (33).

I recommend including two or three portions of soya foods or drinks in a plant-based eating pattern per day. As with any food, we don't want to include too much as this could potentially crowd out other foods and decrease the variety offered to your little one. It is not harmful to give more soya foods than this, but it may mean that you are offering fewer other foods. Similarly, young children should not be offered excessive amounts of cow's milk or dairy products as high intakes have been linked to iron-deficiency anaemia, likely due to the milk or dairy filling them up and resulting in less appetite for other foods, particularly those rich in iron.

One portion of soya food or drink could be any of the following:

125-150ml fortified soya drink

125-150g fortified soya yoghurt

30-35g tofu

50g edamame beans

MEAT ALTERNATIVES

Meat alternatives are usually made from soya, pea, wheat or mushroom protein. Mushroom protein is called mycoprotein, made by Quorn® in the UK. These meat substitutes can be shaped into mince, burgers, sausages and meatballs. Some of these meat alternatives have a similar saturated fat content to red meat and more salt when compared to beef or lamb. However, they are also a good source of protein (like red meat) and contain fibre, unlike meat. They are also cholesterol-free. There is huge variation in the nutritional profile of different types of meat alternatives. For example, Quorn® mince contains only 1.7g fat (0.5g saturated fat) per 100g while Quorn® sausages contain 11g fat (1.2g saturated fat) per 100g. A Beyond Burger contains 19g fat and 6g saturated fat per 100g.

Another consideration is that many meat alternative products can contain high levels of salt, which should be limited for young children. In general, the mince-type products tend to be lower in salt than the sausages and burgers. The salt content varies enormously from product to product and depends on the type that you use. For example, Quorn® mince contains 0.14g of salt per 100g while Quorn® sausages contain 1.2g per 100g, and a Beyond Burger contains 0.75g of salt per 100g. Toddlers aged one to three years should eat no more than 2g of salt a day (0.8g sodium) in total and children aged four to six years should eat no more than 3g salt a day (1.2g sodium) (34).

There have been a few research trials looking at meat alternatives compared to red meat and health outcomes in adults. These studies have looked at various measures related to heart health as well as the effects on the gut microbiome. Overall, they found that measures of heart health were improved after the eight-week trial of replacing meat with a meat alternative in adults. Another study looking at the gut microbiome found that there were increased numbers of beneficial bacteria in the group that replaced some of their meat intake with a meat alternative product (35, 36).

I think that meat alternatives can be safely included in a toddler's eating pattern as they provide some variety and are a good source of protein. However, I wouldn't recommend offering them every day. It is important to remember that most meat alternatives are not a good source of iron, which is a priority nutrient for toddlers. Quorn® is a good source of zinc but not iron, for example. Some meat alternatives are fortified with iron though; if this is the case, you will see it listed in the ingredients.

CASE STUDY

Emily came to me about her two-year-old son Ben. Emily and her husband were vegan, and they wanted to bring up their son eating the same foods as them. Emily was not worried about Ben's growth, but she wanted to make sure that he was getting all the nutrition he needed from his foods. Ben was eating a good variety of foods including vegetables, fruits, hummus, pasta, tofu, pesto, avocado, and toast. Emily was also offering Ben an organic almond drink as she did not want him to have any food additives; she had heard that emulsifiers and seed oils were very bad for our health and that the best plant-based drink is one with the fewest ingredients possible. Ben was not taking any supplements.

My Assessment

When I assessed Ben's diet, he was not having enough calcium for his age, which could affect his bone health later in life. He was also not getting enough vitamin B12 or iodine.

A vitamin B12 supplement of 2.5-5µg per day is essential for all plant-based or mostly plant based children (and more for adults). There are no plant foods that contain vitamin B12 unless they are fortified, and even fortified foods are not a very reliable source of B12, especially for toddlers who can be selective in their eating habits from day to day.

Iodine is a nutrient that is not very abundant on a plant-based diet and the only significant source is seaweed which can contain excessive quantities of iodine, so I don't generally recommend it for toddlers. Iodised salt is not widely available in the UK and therefore salt is not a reliable way to provide iodine to children. In addition, we don't want to encourage the use of too much salt.

My Recommendations

* **Change to a calcium-fortified dairy alternative drink.**
* **Introduce a multivitamin and mineral supplement that contains iodine and vitamin B12.**

I think this case illustrates the importance of supplementing appropriately and not following 'wellness trends' relating to unsubstantiated claims. Although there has been research illustrating that some emulsifiers may have the potential to be harmful for gut health, it is still very important to ensure children are getting sufficient calcium sources from their diet to protect their bone health. Only certain emulsifiers – polysorbate 60 and 80, carrageenan, and carboxymethyl cellulose (CMC) – have been found to be potentially harmful, so a dairy alternative that does not include these could be chosen. Calcium-set tofu is another way of providing an excellent source of calcium to children.

Incredible iron!

All types of lentils
All types of beans and chickpeas
Soya beans / edamame
Tofu / tempeh
Iron-fortified cereals eg. Ready Brek, Weetabix
Chia/hemp/flax seeds
Nut butters
Green vegetables such as peas, kale and broccoli
Lentil pasta

Vitamin C Superstars!

Strawberries
Broccoli
Brussel sprouts   Tomatoes
Peppers   Potatoes
                         Kiwi fruit
                         Citrus fruit

Calcium Champions!

Fortified soya/pea/oat drinks
Fortified soya/oat/coconut yoghurts
Fortified breads
Fortified cereals
Low oxalate vegetables - kale, broccoli.
watercress, spring greens
Oranges
Tahini (sesame seed paste)

SHOPPI

Ready
Black b
Tofu
Chickpeas
Bananas
Soya Drink

Meal Planner

week of _4th September_

	Monday	Tuesday	Wednesday	Thursday	Friday	Saturday	Sunday
Breakfast	Porridge + Ready oats	O/N Oats	Toast + Almond butter		Banana + Soya yog.	Tofu Scramble	Pancakes
Snack	Oatcakes + P.B.						
Lunch	Tofu Nuggets	Falafel + Pitta	Black bean burgers		hummus + Cucumber	chickpea burgers	
Snack	fruit + Soya yog.						
Dinner		Dahl	Lentil ragu + spaghetti				
	Soya Drink						

CHAPTER 7
Plant Powered Little Plates

Chapter 7
Plant Powered
Little Plates

This is the practical part, putting together all the concepts from the previous chapters so that you know exactly what to offer your little one and how to create meals that provide the right nutrients across their day and week. It's all about building a balanced, plant powered plate!

Remember that children's appetites can vary enormously from day to day, so please try not to worry if your little one does not eat all the suggested foods each day. The Plant Powered Little Plate is a guide to how much of each food group to offer, but it's important to let your child decide how much they'd like to eat. Try to look at the variety of foods your child has eaten over a few days or a week, as opposed to every meal or day.

I recommend offering small portions initially; you can always offer more food if your child eats everything they've been given. Large amounts of food can be overwhelming for young children. Aim to offer one or two tablespoons of each food for young toddlers and three or four tablespoons for older toddlers (or the equivalent amounts if the food is not spoonable).

Remember, if you are concerned about your child's food intake or growth, please speak with a health professional so that you can get individual advice for your little one. Your GP or health visitor can be helpful as a first port of call, and they may suggest a referral to a children's dietitian.

The Plant Powered Little Plate

The Plant Powered Little Plate, or PPLP, is a visual guide to help you with meal planning for your little one between the ages of one and five years. The PPLP has four food groups, as well as a central section to emphasise the importance of calcium-rich foods for your little one's bone health. Suggested supplements (vitamin B12, iodine, and DHA) are also displayed on the side of the plate.

The food groups in the Plant Powered Little Plate are:

1. Beans, lentils, peas and soya foods

2. Nuts, seeds and oils/fats

3. Grains and starchy foods

4. Fruits and vegetables

You may have seen or heard of The Eatwell Guide, which is a visual guide to healthy, balanced diets in the UK, developed for adults and children over the age of two years. The NHS guidance for The Eatwell Guide states that children between the ages of two and five "should gradually move to eating the same foods as the rest of the family in the proportions shown in the Eatwell Guide" (1). But what about babies and children under the age of two, and children between two and five years of age whose eating patterns are mostly or entirely plant-based? This is why I have designed the Plant Powered Little Plate, to help you with meal planning for children under five.

A Note About Children Under One Year Old

The PPLP is designed to be used as a visual guide for foods offered to children between one and five years of age. For babies under the age of one, breast milk, formula milk or a combination of the two is a very important part of your baby's diet and still provides the majority of their nutrition, especially during the first three months of introducing solids, as your baby is learning and mastering many feeding skills such as biting, chewing and moving food around in their mouth. From the time that you start introducing solids until about one year of age, there is a gradual increase in the food that your little one eats and a gradual decrease in the amount of milk feeds your baby takes. This process means that by the time they are about one year old, most of your little one's nutrition is coming from foods and a smaller amount from breast milk or a fortified dairy alternative drink (or full-fat cow's milk if your family includes dairy products).

The Plant Powered Little Plate

Beans, Lentils & Soya Foods

Nuts, Seeds & Oils

Calcium-Rich Foods

Grains & Starchy Foods

Fruit & Vegetables

Supplements
Vitamin B12, Iodine, DHA

What is the difference between healthy eating plates for adults and the Plant Powered Little Plate?

There are a few differences between healthy eating guides for older children and adults and the PPLP, which is designed for under-fives. Firstly, the energy density of the diet needs to be higher for young children. You may have noticed that most of the healthy eating guides designed for older children and adults usually recommend around half of the plate to be filled with fruits and vegetables. However, you will see that the fruit and vegetable food group of the PPLP covers around one third of the plate. This is because young children need plenty of energy-rich foods in order to obtain enough calories to support their growth and development. Of course, fruits and vegetables provide important vitamins and minerals, but they are generally fairly low in calories (in other words, their energy density is low). So, we don't want children filling their tummies with too many fruits and vegetables and not leaving enough space for more energy-dense foods.

Secondly, there is more of an emphasis on fats in the PPLP. Young children need more fats than adults as a percentage of their total calories. Practically, what this means is offering a source of fats from nut butters or ground nuts, seeds, avocado, and oils or spreads at most meals and snacks.

Thirdly, I have placed calcium-rich foods at the centre of the PPLP to emphasise the importance of calcium in young children's eating patterns. Several studies have shown that vegan children have lower calcium intakes than vegetarian and omnivorous children, and it is important to ensure that young children are being offered sufficient sources of calcium to protect their bone health. Fortified dairy alternative drinks or yoghurts are an easy and convenient way to offer a concentrated form of bioavailable (easily absorbed) calcium. If your family is vegetarian and you include dairy products, then of course you can offer these as a source of calcium.

Important nutrients and where to find them in the Plant Powered Little Plate

Incredible Iron

Iron-rich foods should be prioritised due to the high iron requirements of babies and toddlers. Iron-rich foods can be found in all four food groups, but particularly good sources of iron include beans, lentils, soya foods, and foods within the grains and starchy foods group. Some green vegetables such as spinach, kale, broccoli, spring greens, and watercress are also fairly good sources of iron. Nuts and seeds contain iron too, particularly cashew nuts, pine nuts, sunflower seeds, and sesame seeds or tahini. Our absorption of iron from plant sources is not as good as it is from animal sources but there are ways to enhance this which I have summarised below (2).

Iron Enhancers

Vitamin C can increase our absorption of iron by two to four times, so it is definitely worth pairing iron-rich foods with those rich in vitamin C whenever possible (3). Some other vitamins, including beta-carotene (the plant-based version of vitamin A), also increase the absorption of iron, so it is always worth adding some colour to your little one's plate (4). Sources of vitamin C include strawberries, kiwi fruit, citrus fruit, blackcurrants, broccoli, potatoes, tomatoes, brussels sprouts, and peppers. Beta-carotene can be found in carrots, mangoes, apricots, and red, yellow and orange peppers.

O-Mazing Omega-3

Foods rich in Omega-3 are mainly found in the nuts, seeds and oils section of the PPLP. Particularly good sources of plant-based omega-3 fats include walnuts and chia, flax and hemp seeds (and their oils) as well as tofu from the beans, lentils and soya foods section. Remember, a supplement of DHA (which is a type of omega-3 fat) is also recommended for pregnant and breastfeeding women and babies and children under the age of two (see Chapter 4 for further details).

FOOD GROUPS IN THE PLANT POWERED LITTLE PLATE

1. FRUITS AND VEGETABLES

Focus on offering as much VARIETY as you can: think lots of different colours and "eating the rainbow". It may sound like a cliché, but eating lots of different coloured fruits and vegetables means that your little one will be obtaining many different vitamins, minerals and phytonutrients. It is also much more fun for your little one to have colourful food as part of their meal! Aim to offer something colourful at most meals and snacks. Here are some examples in the following table.

COLOUR	EXAMPLES OF FOODS	NUTRIENTS
Purple	Grapes, plums, blueberries, aubergine, blackberries, figs, beetroot	Vitamin C, Vitamin K, Vitamin B6, potassium, manganese
Red	Red cabbage, red peppers, tomatoes, red onions, watermelon, raspberries, strawberries, rhubarb, pomegranate, cherries	Vitamin C, Vitamin K, Vitamin A*, potassium
Orange	Orange peppers, oranges, peaches, nectarines, carrots, mangoes, sweet potatoes, papaya, satsumas, squash	Vitamin C, Vitamin A*, folic acid, potassium
Yellow	Yellow peppers, sweetcorn, lemons, bananas, pineapple	Vitamin C, Vitamin A*
White	Onions, garlic, mushrooms, cauliflower, potatoes, ginger, parsnips, turnip	Vitamin C, potassium
Green (there are LOADS!)	Courgettes, broccoli, kale, kiwi fruit, green beans, spinach, brussels sprouts, avocados, lettuce, cucumber, celery	Vitamin C, Vitamin K, folic acid, magnesium, potassium, Vitamin A*

*Plants contain beta-carotene which is converted to vitamin A in the body.

2. GRAINS AND STARCHY FOODS

This food group provides an excellent source of energy and carbohydrates for children, as well as B vitamins, fibre (in wholegrains), protein, and minerals (particularly iron and zinc). Children need at least half of their calories provided by carbohydrates, so this food group is very important. Examples of grains include oats, wheat (within pasta, couscous, bulgur wheat, and bread), millet, rice, potatoes, pearl barley, buckwheat, rye, corn, and quinoa. Starchy foods include potatoes, corn, and sweet potatoes. Offer one of these foods at most meals and some snacks to make sure your little one is getting enough energy throughout the day. I recommend a mix of refined (white) and wholegrain cereals for babies and young children, as too much fibre can fill up small tummies too quickly.

3. LENTILS, BEANS, PEAS AND SOYA FOODS

This food group is a particularly important source of protein, iron and zinc for young children. These are key nutrients, so aim to offer at least one food from this group at all meals. Examples include green, red and brown lentils, black beans, butter beans, chickpeas, borlotti beans, cannellini beans, peanuts, peas, red kidney beans, tofu, soya beans, tempeh, and edamame.

4. NUTS, SEEDS, OILS AND FATS

This food group is a particularly important source of fats and energy, as well as providing significant amounts of protein, vitamins and minerals such as vitamin E, magnesium, selenium and zinc. Nuts and seeds contain mostly unsaturated fats (polyunsaturated and monounsaturated) which are known to be protective for our long-term health, such as the prevention of heart disease. This food group also provides essential fats in the form of alpha-linolenic acid (ALA) and linoleic acid (LA). Particularly good sources of ALA include walnuts and chia, hemp and flax seeds, plus their oils.

Examples of this food group include the following:

- Tree nuts (in the form of nut butters or ground nuts for young children) such as almonds, cashews, walnuts, macadamia nuts, Brazil nuts, pistachios, hazelnuts, pecans, and pine nuts.

- Seeds (sunflower and pumpkin should be offered in the form of seed butters or ground seeds for young children) such as pumpkin, sesame, sunflower, chia, hemp, and flax (also called linseeds).

- Oils and fats such as olive oil, rapeseed oil, avocado oil, and sesame oil as well as fat spreads.

5. CALCIUM-RICH FOODS

This food group is obviously a good source of calcium, but other nutrients provided include protein (from dairy, soya and pea-based foods) and fats: always opt for full-fat varieties, particularly for children under two years of age. Examples of calcium-rich foods include breast milk, fortified dairy alternative drinks made with soya, pea or oat, fortified dairy alternative yoghurts, and calcium-set tofu, as well as cow's milk and dairy products if your family is vegetarian and includes these in their eating pattern. Aim to offer three portions of calcium-rich foods or drinks to one- to-three-year-olds (350mg of calcium per day) and four portions to four- to six-year-olds (450mg of calcium per day).

One portion of calcium-rich food is equivalent to any of the following:

Three or four breast milk feeds per day*

100-120ml cow's milk or fortified dairy alternative drink

100-120g yoghurt or fortified dairy alternative yoghurt

15-20g cheese or fortified dairy alternative cheese**

*With breastfeeding, of course we do not know exactly what volume of milk toddlers are drinking, but if your little one is feeding three or four times a day, I'd recommend offering one or two portions of dairy or fortified dairy alternative products in addition to breastfeeding.

**Note that most plant-based 'cheese' is not fortified with calcium so always check the label. In addition, most cheese and vegan cheese is very high in salt, so I'd recommend small amounts and not offering this to your little one every day.

See the section on calcium in Chapter 6 for more details and refer to the supplements table on page 94 in Chapter 4 for a summary of recommended nutrients for plant-based children.

How to Plan Meals and Snacks for Plant Powered Little People

Daily Checklist

Iron-rich foods (x3)

Calcium-rich foods (x3) for ages 1-3 / (x4) for ages 4-6

Vitamin-rich foods: a fruit and/or vegetable at each meal and snack (x5)

Omega-3 rich foods (x2)

Supplements: vitamin B12, iodine and DHA

Meal Planning Tips

FOR BABIES UNDER ONE:

Continue breastfeeding on demand or offer at least 600ml of formula for ages 7-9 months per day / 400-500ml for ages 10-12 months per day

Babies under 12 months of age generally don't need snacks

Prioritise iron-rich foods paired with vitamin C-rich foods

Prioritise foods high in fats such as nut butter or ground nuts, ground seeds or seed butters

FOR ONE- TO FOUR-YEAR-OLDS:

Continue to breastfeed for as long as you and your toddler would like to

Opt for a calcium-fortified dairy alternative drink or yoghurt (if you don't include dairy products)

Aim to include 3-4 food groups at each meal

Remember to offer at least one iron-rich food at each meal

Example Meals

Peanut butter on toast with strawberries

Black bean dip in a wrap with avocado and tomatoes

Tofu and broccoli stir-fry with noodles and peanut butter sauce

Hummus, pitta bread and cucumber sticks

Tips For Planning Snacks

Aim to include 2-3 food groups within each snack

Aim to offer a fortified dairy alternative drink or yoghurt once a day

Snacks are generally not recommended for babies under 12 months

Example Snacks

Fortified soya yoghurt with sliced fruit

Oatcakes with almond butter and apple slices

Mashed avocado on rice or lentil cakes

Fortified soya/pea/oat drink with a satsuma

EXAMPLE MEAL PLANS FOR PLANT POWERED BABIES

BABIES (8-12 MONTHS)

Babies under 12 months don't need snacks. Offer breastfeeds on demand or around 600ml of formula each day, in addition to the meals suggested below (note that at 11-12 months of age they may be drinking slightly less formula, around 400-500ml each day). Please note that the portion sizes here are a guide; allow your baby to decide how much they would like to eat on any given day as appetites will vary – some days your baby will eat more and other days they may eat less.

BREAKFAST OPTIONS

½-1 iron-fortified wheat biscuit (such as Weetabix or supermarket own-brand)

100ml fortified dairy alternative drink

Raspberries

OR

½-1 slice of bread, lightly toasted

1 heaped teaspoon peanut butter

1-2 tbsp fortified dairy alternative yoghurt

Banana slices (or any fruit)

OR

15g or 4 tbsp iron-fortified Ready Oats

100ml fortified dairy alternative drink

1 heaped teaspoon peanut butter (or tree nut butter such as almond)

½-1 kiwi fruit

LUNCH

25-50g tofu fingers

40g sweet potato roasted with olive or rapeseed oil

1-2 steamed broccoli florets

DINNER

1 lentil burger, cut into strips (see my recipe on page 190)

1-2 avocado slices

1-2 tbsp fortified dairy alternative yoghurt

1-2 ripe strawberries

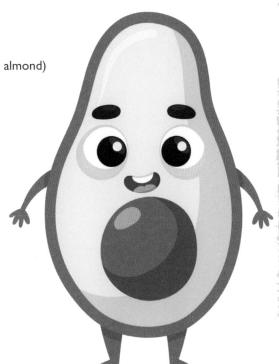

Example meal plans for plant powered toddlers

TODDLERS (1-4 YEARS)

All the quantities given here are approximate; you can offer the suggested amount to your toddler and if they would like more, you can offer more. Some days your toddler may eat less and some days they may eat more as appetites vary from day to day, so please do not worry if your toddler does not always eat the suggested quantities. For fortified dairy alternative drinks, try to choose ones that are unsweetened and fortified with calcium, vitamin D, iodine, vitamin B12, and vitamin B2. Use the 'EPIC-V' guidance on page 136 in Chapter 6 to help choose dairy alternative drinks for your toddler.

BREAKFAST

5-8 tbsp porridge oats (see my porridge and overnight oats recipes on pages 166 and 168)

100-150ml fortified dairy alternative drink

1 teaspoon nut butter or ground nuts

Sliced fruit such as kiwi

SNACK

1-2 oat cakes

1-2 teaspoons cashew butter

LUNCH

1-2 black bean and sweet potato burgers (see my recipe on page 182)

1-2 steamed broccoli florets

3-4 avocado slices

SNACK

125g fortified dairy alternative yoghurt

Sliced fruit such as mango

DINNER

2-4 falafels

1-2 tbsp hummus

½-1 pitta bread

3-4 cucumber slices

BEDTIME (OPTIONAL)

Some toddlers may like to have a breastfeed or a fortified dairy alternative drink (offer 100-200ml).

Suggested Weekly Meal Plan

	MONDAY	TUESDAY	WEDNESDAY	THURSDAY	FRIDAY	SATURDAY	SUNDAY
BREAKFAST	Ready Brek porridge with fortified soya milk, ground nuts or seeds and fruit	Toast with nut butter Fruit and soya yoghurt	Wheat biscuit cereal with soya milk, nut butter or ground nuts or seeds and fruit	Hummus on toast with fruit	Super seeded breakfast cookies Fruit	Ready Brek pancakes with nut butter, blueberries and soya yoghurt	Tofu scramble with fried mushrooms on toast Strawberries
SNACK (OPTIONAL)	Oat cakes with cashew butter	White bean hummus and carrot sticks	Toast with almond butter	Soya yoghurt	Cup of soya milk and fruit	Sliced pepper, guacamole and rice cakes	Oat cakes with hummus
LUNCH	Black bean and sweet potato burgers, broccoli, and avocado	Lentil and carrot fritters Fruit	Chickpea and spinach curry with rice Strawberries	Tofu fingers with roasted sweet potatoes and brussels sprouts	Peanut butter sandwich Fruit and veggies	Mushroom and lentil meatballs with pasta and broccoli	Veggie lasagne with tomatoes and cucumber
SNACK	Cup of soya milk and fruit	Savoury muffin	Cup of soya milk and fruit	Vegan scone and fruit	Savoury muffin	Cup of soya milk and fruit	Soya yoghurt and fruit
DINNER	Falafel and hummus, pitta bread, tomato and cucumber Orange slices	Tofu fingers with potato wedges and roasted peppers	Veggie Bolognese with spaghetti and cauliflower Orange slices	Lentil and quinoa meatballs with broccoli Kiwi fruit	Mild veggie chilli with a tortilla wrap, guacamole and coconut yoghurt	Chickpea burger in a bun with lettuce, tomato, and cucumber	Lentil pasta with homemade pesto Kiwi fruit

Breakfasts

Banana Oat Pancakes

**SERVINGS: 8 PANCAKES | NUTRIENTS: 1.4MG IRON PER PANCAKE
(AROUND ¹/₅ OF A TODDLER'S DAILY IRON REQUIREMENT)**

Pancakes are a wonderful finger food option for babies as they are soft and a great shape to hold if you cut them into strips. They are the perfect breakfast or snack for toddlers too! Using Ready Oats makes the recipe even more nutritious as they are fortified with calcium, iron and vitamins.

INGREDIENTS

125g self-raising flour

60g Ready Oats

2 tbsp ground flaxseed

1 tsp baking powder

1 tsp ground cinnamon

1 large banana, mashed

350ml dairy alternative drink

2 tbsp (30ml) vegetable oil, plus more for frying

METHOD

1. Measure the dry ingredients into a large bowl and mix. In a separate bowl, mix the mashed banana with the dairy alternative drink and vegetable oil.

2. Pour the banana mixture into the dry ingredients and mix with a wooden spoon until the batter is smooth. It should be quite thick.

3. Add spoonfuls of the pancake batter to a frying pan greased with a little oil on a medium heat. When the mixture starts to bubble, turn the pancakes over with a palette knife and cook for about 2 minutes until golden brown and cooked through.

4. Serve the pancakes topped with fruit and nut butter of your choice. They are delicious with peanut butter and sliced banana!

Notes

These pancakes make a nutritious breakfast but can also be enjoyed as a snack on the go.

Once cooked and cooled, the pancakes can be frozen for an easy 'grab and go' snack or breakfast.

Ready Brek is one brand of 'ready oats' but there are many supermarket own brands that are also fortified with iron, calcium and vitamins. You can find these at Sainsbury's, ASDA, Tesco and Aldi.

Add an optional drizzle of honey or maple syrup for toddlers (not appropriate for babies under 12 months of age).

Creamy Strawberry Tofu

SERVINGS: 6 TODDLER PORTIONS

Calcium is a key nutrient for all young children and plant-based eating patterns can be lower in calcium if dairy products are not included. However, calcium-set tofu is a fantastic source of calcium and therefore a great food to include regularly for your little one. This recipe uses calcium-set silken tofu, so it's a fantastic source of calcium and has a super creamy texture too.

Ingredients

180g frozen strawberries

1 block of silken tofu (349g)

1 tbsp maple syrup or honey (optional)

Method

1. Remove the strawberries from the freezer and allow them to thaw for about 1 hour.
2. Add all the ingredients to a blender and blend until smooth.
3. Enjoy as a delicious breakfast or dessert.

Notes

Leave out the maple syrup or honey for children under 1 year of age.

You could use other frozen fruit instead of the strawberries such as mango, mixed berries or banana.

To find out if your brand of tofu is calcium-set, look for calcium sulphate, calcium chloride or E509 as the firming agent in the ingredients list.

If your tofu says 'nigari' in the ingredients list, it is made from magnesium salts and is not calcium-set. You can still use this type of tofu in the recipe, but it will not contain as much calcium.

Calcium-set tofu typically contains 400-500mg calcium per 100g, whereas nigari tofu typically contains around 150mg calcium per 100g.

Green Pancakes

These are such a great option for a savoury breakfast. They can also be offered at any meal or as a snack on the go. I like to serve them with slices of avocado and cherry tomatoes (see notes).

Ingredients

50g spinach, wilted and drained

200ml dairy alternative drink

125g self-raising flour

1 tsp baking powder

1 tbsp flaxseed

1 tsp ground coriander

1 tbsp olive oil

1 avocado

12 cherry tomatoes or 2-3 large tomatoes

Method

1. Blend the spinach and dairy alternative drink together in a blender. Meanwhile, measure the dry ingredients into a bowl.

2. Add the spinach mixture to the dry ingredients and whisk together until you have a smooth and thick batter.

3. Heat the oil in a frying pan on a medium heat, then add spoonfuls of the batter. When the mixture starts to bubble, turn the pancakes over with a palette knife and cook for about 2 minutes until cooked through.

4. Serve the pancakes with slices of avocado and quartered cherry tomatoes on top.

Notes

Remember that whole cherry tomatoes are a choking hazard for under-fives so always serve them cut up into quarters.

For early eaters (six to nine months), serve the pancakes cut into strips with large wedges of tomato, as young babies will not have developed the pincer grasp to pick up smaller pieces of food yet.

Iron Boosted Overnight Oats

SERVINGS: 4 TODDLER PORTIONS OR 2 ADULT PORTIONS | NUTRIENTS: 1.6MG IRON PER TODDLER PORTION (AROUND ¼ OF A TODDLER'S DAILY IRON REQUIREMENT)

The iron-fortified cereal and chia seeds in this recipe both give overnight oats an extra iron boost. Iron is a priority nutrient for babies and toddlers because the iron stores they are born with start to deplete from around six months of age, therefore additional iron needs to be provided in their food. This recipe also includes peanut butter, as peanuts are one of the top nine allergens that we recommend introducing within the first year of life and continuing to offer on a weekly basis, if possible, to help with the prevention of peanut allergies. These overnight oats are a great way of incorporating peanut butter into your little one's eating pattern.

Ingredients

50g porridge oats

1 Weetabix (20g) or a similar supermarket own brand cereal

1 tbsp chia seeds

1 tsp ground cinnamon

250ml fortified dairy alternative drink

50g strawberries or raspberries

1 tbsp peanut butter

Method

1. Combine all the dry ingredients in a clean jar with a lid.

2. Add the dairy alternative drink and stir to combine thoroughly with the dry ingredients.

3. Top with the fruit and refrigerate overnight.

4. In the morning, remove from the fridge and spoon into a bowl.

5. Add the peanut butter to the overnight oats as a topping and enjoy!

Notes

You can use frozen strawberries or raspberries if fresh are not in season, plus they are a lot cheaper!

You can add a little more dairy alternative drink to the oat mixture if it's too thick for your liking.

You can vary the nut butter you use to top the overnight oats, so that your little one has a variety of nuts in their diet. Try almond or cashew butter as well as the peanut butter used here.

Add an optional drizzle of honey or maple syrup for toddlers (not appropriate for babies under 12 months of age).

Iron Boosted Porridge

SERVINGS: 8 TODDLER PORTIONS OR 4 ADULT PORTIONS
NUTRIENTS: 2.2MG IRON PER TODDLER PORTION (AROUND ⅓ OF A TODDLER'S DAILY IRON REQUIREMENT)

In Chapters 5 and 6, I talk about the importance of iron for babies from six months of age and toddlers. Iron requirements increase dramatically from seven months of age because the iron stores that babies are born with start depleting in conjunction with a time of rapid growth. During the toddler years, iron continues to be a very important nutrient and toddlers have high requirements relative to their size. This porridge is 'iron boosted' as it includes iron-fortified oats as well as seeds to increase the iron content. I recommend serving it with fruit and have suggested some toppings below; vitamins A and C from these fruits will improve the absorption of iron.

INGREDIENTS

150g porridge oats
60g Ready Oats (fortified with iron)
1 tbsp hemp seeds
1 tbsp chia seeds
1 tbsp flaxseed
700ml fortified dairy alternative drink (I recommend soya, pea or oat)
1 tbsp peanut butter (or any other nut butter)
1 tbsp ground cinnamon

SUGGESTED TOPPINGS

Grated carrot
Grated apple
Kiwi fruit
Chopped apricots or mango
Berries such as strawberries, blueberries, blackcurrants, or raspberries
Citrus fruit segments such as satsuma, orange, or grapefruit (membrane removed)

METHOD

1. Combine the porridge oats, Ready Oats and all the seeds in a large saucepan on a medium heat. Slowly add the dairy alternative drink and stir to combine.

2. Bring the porridge to the boil, stirring continuously, then mix in the peanut butter and cinnamon (or your other chosen flavourings) until incorporated smoothly.

3. Turn the heat down and simmer until the porridge thickens. You can add a splash of the dairy alternative drink if it becomes too thick.

4. Spoon the porridge into bowls and add your chosen toppings to serve.

Notes

If you can get quinoa flakes, they contain even more iron than oats and you can substitute them for the porridge oats in this recipe. Quinoa flakes are available in health food shops.

You can use cow's milk instead of the dairy alternative drink if your family is vegetarian and includes dairy products in their diet.

This porridge is quite thick, so if you prefer yours a little looser, you can add some more dairy alternative drink to your portion or top it with a dollop of your preferred yoghurt.

Pumpkin Fritters

SERVINGS: 5-6 FRITTERS

This is a very nostalgic recipe for me as it's a version of my mum's pumpkin fritters, which she used to make for us when I was growing up in Cape Town. My mum taught me how to cook and played a huge role in my interest in studying nutrition and becoming a dietitian.

Ingredients

250g pumpkin

1 tsp ground cinnamon

½ tsp allspice

65g self-raising flour

1 tbsp ground flaxseed

1 tbsp brown sugar (optional)

2 tbsp (30ml) dairy alternative drink

Vegetable oil, for frying

Fortified soya yoghurt

Slices of peach or mango

Method

1. Peel and dice the pumpkin, then cook in a large saucepan of boiling water for 20-25 minutes until soft. Drain and leave to cool.

2. Add the cinnamon and allspice to the pumpkin, then mash together until smooth. Gently fold in the flour, flaxseed, and brown sugar until combined.

3. Add the dairy alternative drink to the pumpkin mixture and stir until smooth. The batter should be quite thick.

4. Heat a little vegetable oil in a frying pan over a medium heat. Add spoonfuls of batter to the pan and cook for 2 minutes on each side until golden brown and cooked through.

5. Serve the fritters with a dollop of soya yoghurt and the mango or peach slices on top. If you like, sprinkle them with some extra ground cinnamon too.

Notes

You can use frozen chunks of butternut squash or pumpkin for this recipe if you don't have fresh (and it is so much easier than peeling and chopping a whole pumpkin!).

Leave out the sugar for babies under 12 months of age.

Scrambled Tofu Breakfast Wraps

This is a great recipe for any meal; it can be served for breakfast, lunch or dinner! It's a lovely savoury breakfast and would be great for a packed lunch.

INGREDIENTS

250g firm tofu

2 tsp olive oil

1 onion, finely chopped

½ tsp garlic powder

½ tsp ground turmeric

1 tsp smoked paprika

1 tsp ground cumin

100g cherry tomatoes

3 large or 6 mini tortilla wraps

10g flat leaf parsley

METHOD

1. Remove the tofu from its packaging and squeeze out the water by pressing the tofu with a tea towel (or tofu press if you have one).

2. Heat 1 teaspoon of the olive oil in a frying pan over a medium heat, then add the onion and cook for 2-3 minutes until soft.

3. Add the garlic powder and cook for another minute, then crumble the tofu into the pan and cook for 2 minutes.

4. Add the turmeric, paprika and cumin to the tofu and stir to combine. Cook for another 2 minutes. Meanwhile, cut the cherry tomatoes lengthways into quarters.

5. Transfer the scrambled tofu to a bowl and heat the remaining olive oil in the pan. Cook the cherry tomatoes for 2-3 minutes, then add them to the tofu mixture.

6. Spoon the scrambled tofu and tomato onto the wraps. Finely chop the parsley, sprinkle it over the filling, then fold up the wraps to serve.

Notes

For babies between six and nine months, you could offer the tofu as a finger food by cutting the block into fingers (you can still add the spices). You could also offer the crumbled tofu from a spoon.

From around nine to ten months of age, you could give babies a 'deconstructed' version of this wrap by offering them the scrambled tofu, quartered tomatoes and strips of tortilla wrap separately.

Super Seeded Breakfast Cookies

These are a fantastic option for breakfast as they are packed with nutrition from the oats and seeds. They would also make a great snack on the go for your little one.

Ingredients

100g porridge oats

60g Ready Oats or oat flour

35g pumpkin and sunflower seeds (optional)

1 tbsp chia seeds

1 tbsp flaxseed

1 tsp ground cinnamon

½ tsp baking powder

½ tsp mixed spice

1 carrot, grated

2 bananas, mashed

60ml dairy alternative drink

1 tbsp honey or maple syrup (optional)

Method

1. Preheat the oven to 180°c. Measure all the dry ingredients into a bowl.

2. Add the wet ingredients and mix until it all comes together.

3. Shape the cookie dough into balls and place on a non-stick or lined baking sheet.

4. Bake in the preheated oven for 15 minutes or until golden brown.

Notes

Leave out the honey or maple syrup if you are offering these cookies to babies under one year old.

Use ground seeds for under-ones instead of pumpkin and sunflower seeds, as these large seeds are a choking hazard. Alternatively, just leave the pumpkin and sunflower seeds out.

Toppings For Toast

Toast is a fantastic vehicle for offering foods to your little one that they may not want to eat from a spoon, or that you'd like to offer as a 'baby-led weaning' option. Some examples include black bean dip, hummus, nut butters, and mashed avocado, but I've given lots of ideas to start with here.

Suggested Combinations

Peanut butter with strawberry slices

Cashew butter with kiwi fruit slices

Almond butter with raspberries

Hummus with orange slices

Green Hummus with slices of red pepper

Black Bean Dip with tomato (see notes)

Mashed avocado with tofu, plus a squeeze of lime juice for vitamin C

Notes

The fruit and vegetables suggested here are rich in vitamin C to help with iron absorption.

For young babies aged six to nine months, offer large tomato wedges. For babies around nine to ten months and toddlers, you can offer cherry tomatoes cut into quarters.

You can find my recipes for Black Bean Dip and Green Hummus on pages 230 and 232.

Main Meals

Baby's First Dal

SERVINGS: 8 TODDLER PORTIONS OR 4 ADULT PORTIONS

Dal is honestly one of my favourite meals; it is just so delicious and easy to make. It is also super baby and child friendly as it has a lovely creamy texture and mild spices. It is also a great recipe to batch cook and freeze the leftovers.

Ingredients

100g yellow split peas

200g red lentils

1 tsp ground turmeric

1 tbsp vegetable oil

1 large onion, finely chopped

2 cloves of garlic, crushed

2cm fresh ginger, finely chopped or crushed

1 tsp ground coriander

1 tsp ground cumin

½ tsp ground cinnamon

1 tbsp tomato paste

100ml coconut milk

300g cooked basmati rice

100g cherry tomatoes, quartered

10g fresh coriander, finely chopped

Method

1. Add the yellow split peas to a saucepan with 500ml of cold water and bring to the boil, then simmer for 40 minutes until soft. Drain and set aside.

2. Add the lentils to the pan along with another 500ml of cold water and the turmeric. Bring to the boil and then simmer for 10 minutes until soft.

3. Place another saucepan on a medium heat and add the oil. Fry the onions for about 5 minutes until soft, then add the garlic and ginger and cook for 2 minutes.

4. Add the spices to the onion, garlic and ginger and cook for 1-2 minutes, then add the cooked lentils and split peas and stir to combine everything.

5. Continue stirring while you add the tomato paste and coconut milk to the mixture. You can add a little more coconut milk if the dal seems too thick or you would like a creamier texture.

6. Serve your dal with the basmati rice, topped with the cherry tomatoes and fresh coriander.

Notes

You can add dried chillies to the dal for more of a kick if serving this to older children and adults.

You can also add an optional ½ teaspoon of salt, for adults and older children only. Use a ¼ teaspoon of salt for toddlers and leave out the salt entirely for babies under 12 months of age.

You can double the quantities of this recipe and freeze the other half for an easy and delicious meal to warm up when you are short of time.

Important

Remember that whole cherry tomatoes are a choking hazard, so please cut the cherry tomatoes into quarters for babies from nine to ten months of age and toddlers.

For young babies (six to nine months), I'd recommend serving the dal and rice from a spoon, with large wedges of tomatoes on the side. This is because larger pieces of food are safer for young babies and easier for them to pick up with their fist (called the palmar grasp).

Black Bean and Sweet Potato Burgers

SERVINGS: 5 LARGE OR 10 MINI BURGERS

How do you serve black beans to babies? This is a common question I am asked about all beans; young babies cannot pick up individual beans until they have developed their pincer grasp (usually from around nine to ten months of age). This recipe is perfect for babies from six months as the black beans are mashed with sweet potato and can easily be picked up by little hands. The burgers make perfect finger food cut into strips, or can be served whole for toddlers and older children in a bun.

INGREDIENTS

350g sweet potatoes

1 tbsp + 2 tsp olive oil

1 onion, finely chopped

2 cloves of garlic, crushed

1 x 400g tin of black beans, drained and rinsed

30g plain flour

1 tbsp chia seeds

1 tsp ground cumin

TO SERVE

5 burger buns

1 avocado, sliced

METHOD

1. Preheat the oven to 180°c. Peel the sweet potatoes and chop into 3-5cm cubes.

2. Spread the sweet potato out in a roasting tin, drizzle with the tablespoon of olive oil and roast in the oven for 30-35 minutes until soft. Leave to cool once done.

3. Add 1 teaspoon of olive oil to a frying pan over a medium heat. Fry the chopped onion and crushed garlic for 2-3 minutes until soft and starting to caramelise.

4. Put the cooled sweet potato, fried onion and garlic, black beans, flour, chia seeds, and cumin into a food processor. Pulse until the beans are broken up slightly and the mixture forms a thick dough. If you don't have a food processor, you can simply mash the mixture with a fork.

5. Refrigerate the mixture for about half an hour before shaping into burger patties. Coat your hands with flour so that the mixture doesn't stick to them.

6. Heat the remaining teaspoon of olive oil in a frying pan and cook the burger patties over a medium heat for a few minutes on each side.

7. Cut the burger patties into strips for your baby or serve them in the burger buns for your toddler or older child, alongside the sliced avocado and a vitamin C rich food (such as broccoli, strawberries, peppers and kiwi fruit) to aid iron absorption.

Chickpea Burgers

This meal is one of my family's favourites! It's a great source of iron and plant-based protein in an easy shape for little hands to pick up. It's also a great recipe to get toddlers involved with; they could drain the chickpeas, stir the mixture, squeeze the juice from the lemon or shape the burgers with their hands… The possibilities are endless (and yes there will be a LOT of mess, sorry!).

INGREDIENTS

2 chia eggs (or 2 eggs)

1 x 400g tin of chickpeas, drained and rinsed

1 small bunch of fresh coriander

½ red onion, finely chopped

80g breadcrumbs

Zest of 1 lemon

Juice of ½ lemon

1 tsp ground cumin

Olive oil

TO SERVE

1 large tomato, sliced

4 lettuce leaves

4 burger buns

METHOD

1. First, make the chia eggs unless you are using chicken eggs. To make 1 chia egg, stir 1 tablespoon of chia seeds into 3 tablespoons of water and set aside for about 10 minutes until the mixture has thickened. Repeat as needed.

2. Pour your chia eggs into a food processor, add all the remaining ingredients except the oil and those for serving, then blitz until the mixture comes together. If it looks a little dry, add a tablespoon of water or dairy alternative drink and blend again.

3. Shape the mixture into burger patties (or other shapes such as meatballs) and then chill in the fridge for at least 10 minutes.

4. Add some olive oil to a frying pan and cook the burger patties for a few minutes on each side until golden brown.

5. Top each patty with a large slice of tomato and a lettuce leaf, then serve in a burger bun. Alternatively, slice the burger patties into strips for your baby and serve with a large wedge of tomato (leave out or finely shred the lettuce for babies under 12 months).

Creamy Roasted Pepper Pasta

SERVINGS: 8 TODDLER PORTIONS OR 4 ADULT PORTIONS

If your family is anything like mine, they love pasta! This is a quick and easy recipe for a nourishing pasta sauce. It's similar to pesto but a lot creamier, and a great way to serve cashew nuts to young children.

Ingredients

100g cashew nuts

100ml water

1 red pepper

1 yellow or orange pepper

2 large tomatoes

2-3 cloves of garlic, crushed

1 tbsp olive oil

1 tsp mixed herbs

300g dried lentil or chickpea pasta

Method

1. First, put the cashews in a bowl with the water and set aside to soak. Preheat the oven to 180°c while you chop the peppers and tomatoes into large chunks.

2. Spread the chopped vegetables and crushed garlic out in a large roasting dish and drizzle over the olive oil, then sprinkle over the herbs and mix until coated.

3. Roast the peppers and tomatoes in the preheated oven for 20-25 minutes until soft. Meanwhile, cook the pasta according to the instructions on the packet.

4. Allow the peppers and tomatoes to cool, then combine them with the soaked cashews (including the water) in a food processor.

5. Blend the mixture until a creamy sauce forms, then pour it over the cooked pasta and stir to combine. Once the sauce has warmed through, serve immediately.

Notes

I have suggested lentil or chickpea pasta here to add to the iron content of the overall meal, but you can use any type of pasta for this recipe.

For young babies (six to nine months of age), I'd recommend using large pasta shapes as finger foods such as penne, rigatoni or ziti. Or, you could use smaller pasta shapes and offer them from a spoon.

For babies over nine months who have developed the pincer grasp, you can offer the pasta chopped into smaller pieces.

Green Pasta

This recipe is a great way to offer edamame beans to children as they are blended into the sauce along with the peas.

Ingredients

100g frozen peas

100g frozen edamame beans

200ml dairy alternative drink

10g fresh coriander, plus extra to garnish

1 clove of garlic, crushed

1 lime, zested and juiced

Pinch of ground black pepper

Pinch of salt (optional)

300g dried pasta

Method

1. Boil the peas and edamame beans for 5 minutes until soft, then drain and leave to cool.

2. Put the cooled peas and beans into a blender along with all the other ingredients except the pasta, then blend until smooth.

3. Cook the pasta according to the instructions on the packet and then drain, reserving some of the cooking water.

4. Pour the sauce over the drained pasta, stir to combine and warm it through, then serve.

Notes

I think rigatoni or penne pasta shapes work well with this sauce.

You can use a chickpea or lentil-based pasta to offer a more iron-rich option.

For young babies (six to nine months of age), I'd recommend using large pasta shapes as finger foods such as penne, rigatoni or ziti. Or you could use smaller pasta shapes and offer them from a spoon.

For babies over nine months who have developed the pincer grasp, you can offer the pasta chopped into smaller pieces.

Lentil Burgers

This is a great way to offer lentils to your baby in a finger food format. The smoked paprika, garam masala and garlic granules give them a lovely flavour too; remember that spices are absolutely fine for babies and young children, it is just salt that we need to limit.

INGREDIENTS

1 chia egg (or 1 egg)

1 tsp olive oil

1 onion, finely chopped

1 tsp garlic granules

1 tsp garam masala

1 tsp smoked paprika

1 x 400g tin of green lentils, drained and rinsed

100g oats

TO SERVE

1 large avocado, sliced

1 large tomato, sliced

4 burger buns

METHOD

1. First, make the chia egg unless you are using a chicken egg. To make 1 chia egg, stir 1 tablespoon of chia seeds into 3 tablespoons of water and set aside for about 10 minutes until the mixture has thickened.

2. Add the olive oil to a frying pan over a medium heat. Fry the chopped onion for 2-3 minutes until soft and starting to caramelise, then add the spices and cook for another minute.

3. Pour your chia egg into a food processor, add the lentils, oats and fried onions, then blitz until the mixture comes together but still has some texture.

4. Shape the mixture into burger patties (or other shapes such as meatballs) and then chill in the fridge for at least 10 minutes.

5. Add some olive oil to a frying pan and cook the burger patties for a few minutes on each side until golden brown.

6. Top each patty with a large slice of avocado and tomato, then serve in a burger bun. Alternatively, slice the burger patties into strips for your baby and serve with a large wedge of tomato (leave out or finely shred the lettuce for babies under 12 months).

Notes

Serving these burgers with fruit or vegetables that contain vitamin C will help to aid iron absorption.

Lentil Ragu

This recipe is a real hit with my family and perfect for batch cooking. It is so versatile too, as you can use it as the base for four different meals. I often make a double batch of this recipe on a Sunday and freeze half for another meal later in the week or the following week.

Ingredients

1 tbsp olive oil

1 onion, finely chopped

2 cloves of garlic, crushed

1 tsp smoked paprika

1 tsp ground cumin

1 x 400g tin of green lentils

1 x 250g pouch of Puy lentils

500ml passata

Method

1. Place a large saucepan on a medium heat and add the olive oil. Once the oil is warm, add the onion and cook for 5 minutes until softened.

2. Add the garlic to the onions and fry for another 1-2 minutes, then stir in the smoked paprika and cumin and fry for 1 minute.

3. Add all the lentils to the pan (no need to drain them) and then stir in the passata. Bring to the boil and then simmer for 20 minutes until the sauce thickens.

4. You can now use the ragu in four different ways: as a veggie pie, topped with mashed potato; as a veggie bolognese, served with spaghetti; in a veggie lasagne, layered with béchamel sauce and pasta sheets; or simply as a topping for jacket potatoes.

Notes

To batch cook this recipe, double the quantities and freeze half for another meal later in the week.

You can add some dried chilli to the ragu for adults and older children if you'd like a little extra kick.

In addition to the ideas above, you can serve the lentil ragu on top of foods that are easy for your baby to scoop up, such as mashed potatoes – either let your baby scoop with their hands or pre-load a spoon for them.

You can also serve lentils as burger patties: see my lentil burger recipe on page 190.

Mac and Cheeze

SERVINGS: 8 TODDLER PORTIONS OR 4 ADULT PORTIONS

I don't think I have met a child who doesn't like mac and cheese! This is a different version that includes butternut squash and sweet potato in the sauce as well as butter beans, which creates a lovely creamy texture as well as adding plant protein and iron to the recipe.

INGREDIENTS

150g butternut squash

150g sweet potatoes

2 tbsp olive oil

1 tsp dried thyme

1 tsp ground cumin

300g macaroni pasta

1 large onion, chopped

2 cloves of garlic, crushed

1 x 400g tin of butter beans, drained

3 tbsp (12g) nutritional yeast

500ml dairy alternative drink

METHOD

1. Preheat the oven to 180°c while you peel the butternut squash and sweet potatoes. Chop them into 2-3cm cubes and spread out in a large roasting tin, then drizzle with a tablespoon of the olive oil and a sprinkling of the thyme and cumin. Roast in the oven for 30 minutes.

2. Meanwhile, cook the pasta according to the instructions on the packet, then drain. Aim to time this so it's ready when your sauce is done.

3. Heat the remaining oil in a large saucepan, then fry the onion and garlic with the remaining thyme and cumin for a few minutes until the onion is soft.

4. Once the butternut squash and sweet potatoes are roasted and soft, add them to the saucepan with the onion and spices.

5. Stir in the tinned butter beans, nutritional yeast, and dairy alternative drink, then blend the sauce with a handheld blender until smooth.

6. Pour the sauce over the pasta, stir to combine and then serve immediately.

Notes

I think rigatoni or penne pasta shapes work well with this sauce. You can use a chickpea or lentil-based pasta to offer a more iron-rich option.

For young babies (six to nine months of age), I'd recommend using large pasta shapes as finger foods such as penne, rigatoni or ziti. Or you could use small pasta shapes and offer them from a spoon.

For babies over nine months who have developed the pincer grasp, you can offer the pasta chopped into smaller pieces.

Pea and Mint Fritters

I love the flavour combination of peas and fresh mint; they work so well together. Like sweetcorn fritters, these are a great lunchtime meal or lunch box addition.

INGREDIENTS

150g frozen peas

125g self-raising flour

1 tbsp ground flaxseed

10g fresh mint, chopped

1 lime, zested and juiced

200g soya yoghurt

1 tbsp olive oil

METHOD

1. Cover the frozen peas with water in a small bowl, then microwave for 2 minutes until soft.

2. Combine the flour, flaxseed, mint, and lime zest in a large mixing bowl.

3. Add the drained peas, lime juice and soya yoghurt to the bowl, then mix until a thick batter forms.

4. Heat the olive oil in a frying pan, then add spoonfuls of the batter and cook for 2-3 minutes on each side until golden brown.

Notes

I love serving these fritters with hummus and some fruit such as strawberries, kiwi fruit or orange slices, as they are all rich sources of vitamin C to help with iron absorption.

Peanut Noodles with Green Veggies

SERVINGS: 8 TODDLER PORTIONS OR 4 ADULT PORTIONS

This recipe is another family favourite of ours! The combination of the peanut flavour with the edamame beans and broccoli is so delicious. Edamame beans are a great source of protein and iron.

INGREDIENTS

150g dried rice noodles

100g frozen edamame beans

1 onion, chopped

200g broccoli

FOR THE PEANUT SAUCE

60g peanut butter

6 tbsp warm water

2 tbsp soy sauce or coconut aminos*

2 tbsp red wine vinegar

1 tsp garlic powder

1 tsp brown sugar (optional)

METHOD

1. Soak the rice noodles in boiling water for 2-3 minutes. Meanwhile, boil or microwave the frozen edamame beans for 3 minutes.

2. Combine all the ingredients for the peanut sauce in a bowl and whisk together.

3. Fry the onion in a little oil for a few minutes, then add the broccoli and stir fry for 3-4 minutes (depending on how soft or al dente you'd like the broccoli).

4. Pour the peanut sauce into the pan, add the noodles and edamame beans, then stir to combine and let the sauce warm through before serving.

Notes

Leave out the sugar for babies under 12 months of age.

*Coconut aminos is an alternative soya-free option to soy sauce and is very low in salt in comparison to soy sauce, making it suitable for babies.

In order to serve this meal to the youngest members of your family, I'd recommend deconstructing the meal. For babies, mash or flatten the edamame beans and offer them on a spoon.

Peanuts are a common allergen. If this is the first time your baby has had peanuts, refer to Chapter 5 for further information and guidance on introducing allergens.

Rainbow Couscous Salad

I love couscous as it is so versatile and easy to prepare. It also adds a grainy texture to foods to help babies progress with learning about different textures. The vegetables in this salad have been roasted, so they are super soft and easy to offer to the youngest members of your family.

INGREDIENTS

1 red pepper

1 orange pepper

1 yellow pepper

1 red onion

1 tbsp olive oil

100g asparagus

180g couscous

1 x 400g tin of chickpeas, drained and rinsed

75g dairy or vegan feta (optional)

FOR THE DRESSING

Juice of 1 lemon

2 tbsp olive oil

2 cloves of garlic, crushed

Salt and pepper, to taste (optional)

METHOD

1. Preheat the oven to 180°c. Slice the peppers into long strips and chop the red onion into chunks. Spread them out in a large roasting tin and drizzle over the olive oil, then roast for 30 minutes until soft and beginning to blister.

2. After 15-20 minutes, add the asparagus to the tin and roast for the last 10-15 minutes.

3. Meanwhile, put the couscous in a heatproof bowl and cover with boiling water, then leave it to stand for 10 minutes to soften and absorb all the liquid. Fluff with a fork once done.

4. Mix the chickpeas with the couscous in a large serving dish and top with the roasted vegetables.

5. Measure the ingredients for the dressing into a jug and whisk to combine, then pour over the couscous salad to serve.

Notes

For babies, you can offer the couscous from a spoon and serve the roasted vegetables separately as a finger food. Serve with hummus instead of whole chickpeas.

For toddlers, you can offer the salad deconstructed with the roasted vegetables as finger food. Ensure that the chickpeas are squashed or flattened as whole chickpeas are a choking hazard.

Feta is a very salty cheese, so I wouldn't recommend offering it to babies under 12 months of age. Only offer small amounts of feta to toddlers.

Sweetcorn Fritters

This is a great recipe for a lunchtime meal or as an addition to a lunch box. It is perfect for little hands to pick up but equally delicious for adults too. I like to serve the fritters with tofu and fruit to make a complete meal.

INGREDIENTS

1 tin of sweetcorn (165g drained weight)

3 spring onions, sliced

200ml dairy alternative drink

150g self-raising flour

1 tbsp ground flaxseed

1 tsp smoked paprika

1 tbsp olive oil, for frying

OPTIONAL (FOR ADULTS AND OLDER CHILDREN)

Pinch of dried chilli flakes

Pinch of salt

TO SERVE

300g firm tofu

1 orange

METHOD

1. Combine the sweetcorn, spring onion, dairy alternative drink, flour, flaxseed, and smoked paprika in a large mixing bowl, stirring until you have a thick batter.

2. Heat the olive oil in a frying pan over a medium heat, then add spoonfuls of the sweetcorn mixture. Cook the fritters for 2-3 minutes on each side until golden brown.

3. I like to serve these fritters with strips of tofu for protein and iron as well as some fruit such as orange segments (see notes).

Notes

These fritters are perfect for babies from six months of age.

For young babies (six to nine months), serve the orange in large wedges with the skin on and membranes removed. For babies over nine months of age, you can serve the orange cut into smaller pieces with the membranes removed.

Tofu is made from soya beans which are a common allergen. If this is the first time your baby has had soya, refer to Chapter 5 for further information and guidance on introducing allergens.

Tofu Fried Rice

SERVINGS: 8-10 TODDLER PORTIONS OR 4-5 ADULT PORTIONS

My family loves this recipe! As they know, I am always looking for ways to make our meals more colourful and this fried rice ticks that box perfectly. It's also very quick to make and comes together in about 15 minutes, great for weeknight dinners. The recipe includes soy sauce, which I wouldn't recommend for babies under one year of age; see the notes below on serving this meal to your baby.

INGREDIENTS

300g basmati rice

FOR THE TOFU

1 tsp olive oil

250g block of firm tofu

½ tsp ground turmeric

2 tsp smoked paprika

1 tsp garlic powder

FOR THE STIR-FRIED VEGETABLES

1 tsp olive oil

1 onion, finely chopped

1 clove of garlic, crushed

1 large carrot, grated

1 red pepper, chopped

150g frozen peas or edamame beans

1 tbsp soy sauce (optional)

3 spring onions, chopped

METHOD

1. Cook the basmati rice according to the instructions on the packet.
2. Meanwhile, place a saucepan over a medium heat, add the olive oil and then crumble in the tofu. Stir in the turmeric, paprika and garlic powder, then cook for 2-3 minutes.
3. In a large frying pan or wok, heat the olive oil for the stir-fried vegetables until very hot.
4. Add the onion to the frying pan and cook for 5 minutes until soft, then add the garlic and cook for another 1-2 minutes.
5. Add the carrot and pepper to the frying pan and cook until soft, then stir in the peas or edamame and cook for a further 2 minutes.
6. Now add the tofu and cooked rice to the vegetables in the frying pan and stir to combine.
7. Add the soy sauce if using and stir to mix throughout the rice and vegetables.
8. Serve the fried rice topped with the chopped spring onions.

Notes

Tofu is made from soya beans which are a common allergen. If this is the first time your baby has had soya, refer to Chapter 5 for further information and guidance on introducing allergens.

How to serve this meal to babies:

Keep some tofu aside for your baby and cut it into thick strips (you can still add the spices). After the rice has cooked, set some aside and roll into balls with a little avocado or hummus to help the rice stick together. Serve the peas or edamame mashed and from a spoon for young babies (six to nine months) or flattened/squashed for older babies (nine to 12 months).

Make sure the carrots and peppers are cooked until soft, so that your baby can 'mash' them with their gums.

Tofu Nuggets

Crunchy on the outside and soft in the middle: these are so good!

Ingredients

40g plain flour

1 tsp garlic powder

100ml dairy alternative drink

100g breadcrumbs

250g block of firm tofu

2 tbsp vegetable oil

Method

1. Combine the flour and garlic powder in a jug, then add the dairy alternative drink and whisk until smooth. Pour the batter into a shallow bowl.

2. Add the breadcrumbs to another bowl. Pat the tofu until dry and then cut into 2-3cm cubes or tear into chunks.

3. Drop the tofu cubes into the batter and turn to make sure they are fully coated, then dip them into the breadcrumbs and toss to make sure they are fully coated once again.

4. Heat the vegetable oil in a frying pan over a medium heat, then add the tofu to the frying pan and fry for 5 minutes, turning halfway through, until golden brown on all sides.

5. Serve straight away for older children and adults but remember to let the tofu nuggets cool slightly before serving to young children.

Notes

You could add these tofu nuggets to the peanut noodles on page 198 or serve them with potato wedges and peas to complete the meal.

Tofu is made from soya beans which are a common allergen. If this is the first time your baby has had soya, refer to Chapter 5 for further information and guidance on introducing allergens.

Snacks

2 Ingredient Nice Cream

SERVINGS: 2 TODDLER PORTIONS OR 1 ADULT PORTION

This is such a quick and easy recipe. The frozen bananas create such a creamy texture when blended and the peanut flavour is just gorgeous with banana. You could serve this as a dessert or as a snack on a warm day.

INGREDIENTS

1 large ripe banana

1 tbsp peanut butter (or any nut butter)

METHOD

1. Peel and chop the banana, place in a resealable bag and freeze.
2. Take the frozen banana out and leave it to thaw for 5-10 minutes.
3. Add the banana and nut butter to a blender and blend until smooth.

Notes

You can offer this nice cream to babies from a spoon or add a scoop to a cone for a toddler as a fun dessert!

Cheezy Broccoli Muffins

These muffins are a great way to use up broccoli in your fridge, plus the nutritional yeast and mustard give them a 'cheesy' flavour. These are perfect for lunch boxes or as a snack on the go.

INGREDIENTS

300g broccoli

240g self-raising flour

15g nutritional yeast

2 tbsp ground flaxseed

1 tsp baking powder

250ml fortified dairy alternative drink

125ml vegetable oil

1 tbsp Dijon mustard

METHOD

1. Preheat the oven to 180°c. Steam the broccoli for 10 minutes until soft (but not mushy).

2. Combine the self-raising flour, nutritional yeast, flaxseed, and baking powder in a bowl.

3. Roughly chop the steamed broccoli and add it to the dry ingredients. In a jug, whisk the dairy alternative drink, vegetable oil and Dijon mustard together.

4. Add the mixture in the jug to the bowl and gently fold everything together until just combined.

5. Spoon the mixture into a greased muffin tray and bake for 20 minutes until golden brown.

Notes

Nutritional yeast is a very nutritious addition to recipes as it contains B vitamins (vitamin B12 if fortified), protein and zinc. Plus, it gives these muffins a delicious 'cheesy' flavour!

Ice Lollies

SERVINGS: 6 SMALL LOLLIES PER RECIPE

Each of these recipes makes around six lollies and contains only three ingredients!
Simply add all the ingredients to a blender, blend until smooth,
pour into ice lolly moulds and then pop in the freezer.

STRAWBERRY SUNDAE

12 large strawberries

1 large ripe banana

300ml fortified dairy alternative drink

BERRYLICIOUS

A handful of blueberries

1 large ripe banana

300ml fortified dairy alternative drink

TROPICAL SUNSHINE

1 large ripe mango

1 large ripe banana

300ml fortified coconut drink

PEACHES AND CREAM

2 ripe peaches

1 large ripe mango

300ml fortified dairy alternative drink

Notes

You can also add a teaspoon of nut butter before blending to make the lollies
extra creamy. This also adds good fats and extra calories to the lollies.
Ice lollies are great for easing sore gums when babies and toddlers are teething.

Lemon and Blueberry Flapjacks

It is estimated that breastfeeding mums need an additional 300-500 calories each day (especially during the first six months of breastfeeding) in order to support the body to make breast milk. These flapjacks are a fantastic snack for breastfeeding mums or anyone in need of an energy boost!

INGREDIENTS

100g oats

30g sunflower and pumpkin seeds

20g Ready Oats or plain flour

1 tbsp chia seeds

1 tsp ground cinnamon

2 ripe bananas

60ml neutral oil

60ml fortified dairy alternative drink

70g blueberries

1 lemon, zested

METHOD

1. Preheat the oven to 180°c and measure all the dry ingredients into a bowl.

2. In a separate bowl, mash the bananas and then combine them with the oil and dairy alternative drink.

3. Add the banana mixture to the dry ingredients and stir to combine. Stir in the blueberries and lemon zest until they are evenly distributed throughout the mixture.

4. Transfer the mixture to a greased baking tin and flatten with a fork to get an even surface.

5. Bake for 20 minutes until golden brown, then leave to cool before cutting into 12 pieces.

Notes

If you are going to offer these flapjacks to your toddler, use ground seeds or leave out the sunflower and pumpkin seeds as they are a choking hazard.

Lily's Mango Sorbet

Our eldest daughter Lily loves mango and she will always choose sorbet over any other type of ice cream! This is her favourite frozen dessert, which she created for herself.

Ingredients

150g frozen mango

200g frozen pineapple

200ml coconut milk

1 lime, zested and juiced

Method

1. Take the frozen mango and pineapple out the freezer and allow to thaw slightly before placing in a blender with the coconut milk, lime zest and lime juice.

2. Blend until smooth, then transfer the mixture to a freezer-proof container.

3. Freeze overnight. Serve the mango sorbet in a cone for a delicious summer dessert.

Notes

You can either use tinned coconut milk or a fortified coconut drink; the fortified drink will provide more calcium and vitamins.

Nourishing Smoothies for Breastfeeding Mums

SERVINGS: 1 ADULT PORTION PER SMOOTHIE

Breastfeeding mums have high nutritional requirements, especially for calcium as they need 1250mg per day. Each of these smoothies contains around 600mg calcium, which is almost half of your daily calcium requirements in one drink. Simply add all the ingredients to a powerful blender and whizz until smooth, then pour into a glass and enjoy.

GREEN SMOOTHIE

300ml fortified dairy alternative drink

15g Ready Oats

25g spinach

1 banana

1 tsp peanut butter

½ tsp ground cinnamon

TROPICAL SMOOTHIE

300ml fortified dairy alternative drink

15g Ready Oats

50g pineapple

50g mango

1 banana

1 tsp tahini

BERRY SMOOTHIE

300ml fortified dairy alternative drink

15g Ready Oats

100g strawberries

1 banana

1 heaped tsp cashew butter

½ tsp ground cinnamon

Peanut Butter Biscuits

These biscuits contain both chickpeas and peanut butter, so they are fantastic source of fibre, protein, and good fats. They make a delicious and satisfying snack or can be served as a breakfast with some banana on the side.

INGREDIENTS

125g peanut butter

100g oats

30g Ready Oats

1 x 400g tin of chickpeas, drained and rinsed

6 partially rehydrated dates

30ml dairy alternative drink

2 tbsp maple syrup or honey (optional)

METHOD

1. Preheat the oven to 190°c. Put all the ingredients in a food processor and pulse until the mixture comes together.

2. Shape the biscuit dough into balls and place on a baking tray, then flatten each one slightly with the back of a fork.

3. Bake the biscuits in the preheated oven for 20 minutes until golden brown.

Notes

You can use different types of nut butters if you don't have peanut butter or would like to vary the recipe. For example, almond butter or cashew butter would work.

Peanuts are a common allergen. If this is the first time your baby has had peanuts, refer to Chapter 5 for further information and guidance on introducing allergens.

The maple syrup or honey is optional because the biscuits already have some sweetness from the dates. Leave this out if you are offering the biscuits to children under 12 months of age.

Pear and Walnut Muffins

SERVINGS: 12 MUFFINS

These muffins are so delicious and ideal for little hands to pick up. They could be part of a lunch box or as a snack when you are out and about.

Ingredients

240g self-raising flour

100g oats

50g walnuts, finely chopped

1 tsp baking powder

1 tsp ground cinnamon

3-4 ripe pears, chopped

250ml dairy alternative drink

125ml vegetable oil

1 tsp vanilla essence

Method

1. Preheat the oven to 180°c. Measure the flour, oats, walnuts, baking powder, and cinnamon into a large mixing bowl. Stir to combine.

2. Add the chopped pears to the flour mixture and fold in, then add the dairy alternative drink, vegetable oil and vanilla essence. Mix until just combined.

3. Spoon the mixture into a greased muffin tray and bake for 20 minutes until golden brown.

Notes

You could use other fruit such as apples or blueberries in this recipe if you don't have pears.

The walnuts are a fantastic source of the essential omega-3 fat alpha-linolenic acid (ALA).

Spinach and Roasted Pepper Muffins

These savoury muffins are a great addition to lunch boxes, and you can freeze them after cooking to bring out for a quick snack or part of a packed lunch.

INGREDIENTS

1 red pepper, diced

1 orange or yellow pepper, diced

240g self-raising flour

1 tsp baking powder

1 tsp smoked paprika

50g baby spinach, chopped

250ml dairy alternative drink

125ml vegetable oil

Pinch of dried chilli (optional)

METHOD

1. Preheat the oven to 180°c and roast the peppers with a drizzle of olive oil for 20 minutes.

2. Measure the self-raising flour, baking powder and smoked paprika into a bowl and mix.

3. Add the roasted peppers and spinach to the flour mixture, then add the dairy alternative drink and the vegetable oil and stir until just combined. Add the chilli if using.

4. Spoon the mixture into a greased muffin tin and bake in the oven for 20 minutes.

Notes

As an optional extra, you can crumble 75g of feta or a vegan alternative on top of the muffins before baking them.

As feta cheese is quite salty, I recommend not using feta for babies under 12 months of age.

The dried chilli adds a little bit of heat for older children and adults.

Dips

Black Bean Dip

This is a lovely iron-rich dip you can serve to your baby either from a spoon or spread on toast. The dip also contains vitamin C from the lime juice to help with iron absorption.

Ingredients

1 x 400g tin of black beans, drained and rinsed

1 small handful of fresh coriander

1 small red onion, finely chopped

1 lime, zested and juiced

1 tsp garlic powder

1 tsp ground cumin

60ml olive oil

80ml water

Method

1. Add all the ingredients to a blender and blend until smooth.

Notes

Serve from a spoon or spread on toast for your baby. For adults and older children, you can serve the dip with tortilla chips or crackers.

If you like, add a ¼ teaspoon of salt and a pinch of chilli flakes to the dip before blending if serving to older children and adults. Make sure you leave out the salt for children under 12 months of age.

Green Hummus

SERVINGS: 8-10 TODDLER PORTIONS OR 4-5 ADULT PORTIONS

As a variation of the usual chickpea-based dip, here's a green hummus made with edamame beans and peas. It's so tasty and super nutritious: a fantastic source of plant-based iron, protein, good fats, and vitamin C. Suitable from six months onwards.

Ingredients

130g frozen edamame beans

130g frozen peas

2 tbsp tahini

2 tbsp olive oil

1 clove of garlic

1 small bunch of mint

1 lemon, juiced

125ml water

Method

1. Cook the frozen edamame beans and peas for 3-4 minutes until soft, then drain and allow to cool.

2. Add all the ingredients to a blender and blend until smooth. Serve and enjoy!

Notes

You can offer this hummus to your baby from a spoon, spread it on some toast or serve it as a dip for any cooked vegetable.

Maddie's Favourite Cheezy Sauce

Both our daughters enjoy cooking, and this is one of Maddie's favourites! Maddie loves pasta with a creamy sauce, and she learnt how to make this recipe from a young age.

Ingredients

1 tbsp olive oil

1 small red onion, finely chopped

50g plain flour

500ml fortified dairy alternative drink

50g grated cheddar or vegan cheese (optional)

Salt and pepper, to taste

Method

1. Add the olive oil to a saucepan over a medium heat. When the oil is warm, add the onion and fry for 2-3 minutes until soft.

2. Add the flour to the saucepan and stir, then slowly start to add the dairy alternative drink, stirring constantly as you pour it into the saucepan.

3. Continue stirring the sauce until it thickens and then remove from the heat.

4. Add the cheese or vegan cheese, if using, and stir until melted. Otherwise, you can just use the sauce as a creamy white sauce without the cheese.

Notes

This sauce can be used as the béchamel in a veggie lasagne: see my lentil ragu recipe on page 192. It can also be used on its own with some cooked pasta and frozen vegetables, such as peas, or to make cauliflower (or broccoli) cheese as a side dish.

Spiced Hummus

SERVINGS: 8-10 TODDLER PORTIONS OR 4-5 ADULT PORTIONS

Chickpeas are so versatile and nutritious; they are a fantastic source of protein and iron for your plant powered little person! However, whole chickpeas are a choking hazard for little ones, so hummus is a safe way to serve chickpeas to babies and young toddlers. The lemon juice provides a source of vitamin C to help with iron absorption. Suitable from six months onwards.

Ingredients

1 x 400g tin of chickpeas, drained and rinsed

3 tbsp olive oil

2 tbsp tahini

1 lemon, juiced

1-2 cloves of garlic, finely chopped or crushed

1 tsp garam masala

60ml water

Method

1. Put all the ingredients into a blender (I used a Nutribullet) and blend until smooth. That's it!

Notes

You can offer this hummus to your baby from a spoon, spread it on some toast or serve it as a dip for any cooked vegetable.

Instead of chickpeas, you could use butter beans or cannellini beans as a variation. You could also use a nut butter instead of tahini, such as almond, cashew, or peanut butter.

SCAN FOR REFERENCES

You can scan this QR code to read all the references from each chapter.

SCAN ME